HOW TO WORK WITH RUDE, OBNOXIOUS AND APATHETIC KIDS

REACHING OUT TO THE KID WHO DRIVES YOU UP THE WALL

LES CHRISTIE

VICTOR BOOKS

A DIVISION OF SCRIPTURE PRESS PUBLICATIONS INC.
USA CANADA ENGLAND

Revised, updated edition.
Formerly titled:
When You Have to Draw the Line.

All Scripture quotations, unless otherwise indicated, are from the *Holy Bible, New International Version®*. Copyright © 1973, 1978, 1984, by International Bible Society. Used by permission of Zondervan Publishing House. All rights reserved. Verses marked TLB are taken from *The Living Bible*, © 1971, Tyndale House Publishers, Wheaton, IL 60189. Used by permission. Verses marked PH from J.B. Phillips: *The New Testament in Modern English*, Revised Edition, © J. B. Phillips, 1958, 1960, 1972, permission of MacMillan Publishing Co. and Collins Publishers.

Cover design: Scott Rattray

ISBN: 1-56476-351-X

3 4 5 6 7 8 9 10 Printing/Year 98 97 96 95

Produced for Victor Books by the Livingstone Corporation. David Veerman, Michael Kendrick, and Brenda Todd, project staff.

CONTENTS

*This book is fondly dedicated to three delightful, encouraging,
and insightful ladies who typed my original manuscript:
our secretary in the youth department at
Eastside Christian Church, Linda Merold;
a volunteer at that same church, Susan Elliott;
and our faculty secretary at San Jose Christian College, Bonnie Sloan.*

INTRODUCTION

My fourth-grade Sunday School experience was unforgettable. I only attended the church for six months, yet it was one of the triggers that prompted me to write this book. Though I did not become a Christian until years later, this brief stint in church taught me a lot about the effects of inadequate discipline.

The class contained about fourteen fourth, fifth, and sixth graders, over whom our teacher had absolutely no control. Each week featured a different form of chaos. Often Bibles and other materials were thrown around the room. Sometimes students entertained themselves and others with obscene sounds and gestures. It was fun for about ten minutes—until some of us began to fear bodily damage from some of the larger students.

I have often thought how frustrated that poor teacher must have been. The teacher was baffled about what to do with her unruly group. Coming to the end of her rope, she would finally, in absolute despair, let us out early. She may have cared about us (she did remember to send us birthday cards); however, she could never remember our names in class and often had excuses for being unprepared to teach each Sunday. This only made it more difficult to keep our extremely active class under control.

I did have one positive early experience with this church, but it came outside the Sunday School class setting. During the six months I attended, my parents would drop me off and pick me up in front of the church each Sunday. There was one lady who would always be out in front greeting people. She always called me by my name and told me how glad she was that I was there. Each Sunday as I left, she said good-bye to me as I got into my parents' car and invited me back next week. She had a wonderful smile and made me feel extremely welcome.

One particular Sunday, I was leaning against the church wall, watching our church youth minister play ball with some high schoolers, when that friendly lady who knew my name came up to me. I think she sensed my admiration of the youth minister, because she casually asked if I thought the youth minister was a sharp person. I was fairly shy at the time, so looking down, I kicked the ground with my shoe and quietly said, "Yeah." Then she said something I would never forget. She said, "You know, Les, I think someday you'd make a good youth minister!" That was the end of the conversation. My parents arrived, I got into the car, and they took me home. But I never forgot those words.

Humanly speaking, one of the reasons I'm a youth minister today is because one woman (whose name I don't even know) thought I could do it. That incident taught me that adult youth workers can have an enormous influence on young people's lives through positive relationships. Every time I see a young person today I want to say something to encourage him or her, because I can never predict the impact of those words. And that's why this book will emphasize the positive aspects of working with rude, obnoxious, and apathetic youth.

According to Dr. Fitzhugh Dodson's latest (unscientific) count in *How to Discipline with Love,* there are approximately 1,823 books and pamphlets on the subject of discipline.[1] Typically books on discipline are built around a single method of disciplining young people. But there are many inadequacies in a single-system approach.

In every youth group there will be a variety of young people as described by Elizabeth Crisci in *What Do You Do with Joe?*[2] You may come across the Bashful Brooke, Turned-off Tiffany, Know-it-all Nathan, Doubting Debra, Rebellious Ryan, Silly Sarah, Daydreaming Danielle, Troubled Tony, Friendless Fran, Unloved Lindsey, Slow-learner Steven, Domineering Dana, Resentful Roger, and Super-spiritual Scott. There is not one approach that will work at all times with all of these young people. Each young person is unique. With some young people who are causing problems, all you need to do is look at them and they will cry. You can beat others with a steel girder and they won't budge.

The problem of disciplining kids is a hot issue for those of us who work with them. It comes at us from every direction. We're told by our pastors that some of "our kids" have been disrupting the worship services. We have teachers and other leaders resign because of the kids' behavior. We get aggravated ourselves when we try to present a creative program, only to witness what seems like the group coming completely unglued. How can we keep disruptive kids and discipline problems from dominating our ministry to youth?

There are a variety of ways to guide young people within the confines of a youth group. It is my hope that *How to Work with Rude, Obnoxious and Apathetic Kids* will be practical and helpful. With the variety of strategies given, I am confident you will find several that fit the type of youth ministry discipline that suits your style of youth work.

Give any new method mentioned in *How to Work with Rude, Obnoxious and Apathetic Kids* an honest try till you understand it and feel comfortable with it. Any new method is bound to feel strange at first. If you find, after sincere effort, that some recommended method feels foreign and is just not you, drop it and use another method.

Every book I have read on discipline has been geared to the pre-adolescent, with the attitude that teenagers are unmovable, unchangeable, and unbendable. Occasionally I would find a book with a token chapter aimed at the teen years. *How to Work with Rude, Obnoxious, and Apathetic Kids* is designed specifically for those working with junior and senior highers. I strongly believe they are still pliable and moldable at this age. As time moves on they may become set in concrete, but during their teen years we are still working with wet cement.

Howard Hendricks translates Ephesians 6:4; "But bring them up in *chastening* and *instruction* of the Lord." He continues to say that every competent physician practices two forms of medicine—corrective (chastening) medicine and preventive (instructive) medicine.[3] Every good youth worker practices both forms of discipline (corrective and preventive). Unfortunately, many of us define discipline only in the corrective sense. *How to Work with Rude, Obnoxious and Apathetic Kids* is intended to help you deal not only with present situations, but also to help prevent future problems from occurring.

Remember that using the "D" word with your students doesn't mean you have to come down hard on them all the time. It's not an excuse to take out your frustrations on disruptive class members. But discipline is a tool to keep your group situations from disintegrating into chaos and creating confusion that is just as upsetting to students as it is to leaders. Positive discipline provides for a secure learning environment—one that group members will want to return to.

SECTION ONE

"This is our son, Shawn. We'll pick him up when he turns eighteen."

WHEN EVERYTHING NAILED DOWN IS COMING LOOSE

It's not easy being a youth worker or a parent today. You've heard that tune before, right? Well, parenting and youth work are tough jobs—they have been a challenge for a long time. And rough as it is for today's parents and youth workers, they are just taking part in a long tradition passed down by parents of teenagers and youth workers through the ages.

"An angry father asks his teenage son, 'Where did you go?' The boy, as he is trying to sneak home late at night says, 'Nowhere.' 'Grow up,' his father chides him. 'Stop hanging around the public square and wandering up and down the street. Go to school. Night and day you torture me. Night and day you waste your time having fun'" (Translated from 4,000-year-old Sumerian clay tablets).

"I see no hope for the future of our people if they are dependent on the frivolous youth of today. For certainly all youth are reckless beyond words. When I was a boy we were taught to be discreet and respectful of elders, but the present youth are exceedingly wild and impatient" (Ancient Greek poet Hesiod).

"Youth today love luxury. They have bad manners, contempt for authority, no respect for older people, and talk nonsense when they should work. Young people do not stand up any longer when adults enter the room. They contradict their parents, talk too much in company, guzzle their food, lay their legs on the table, and tyrannize their elders" (Socrates).

"The world is passing through troublous times. The young people of today think of nothing but themselves. They have no reverence for parents or old age. They are impatient of all restraint. They talk as if they knew everything, and what passes for wisdom with us is foolishness with them. As for the girls, they are forward and immodest, and unwomanly in speech, behavior, and dress" (Peter the Hermit, A.D. 1274).

"Our earth is degenerate—children no longer obey their parents" (Carved on stone 6,000 years ago by an Egyptian priest).

"From there Elisha went up to Bethel. As he was walking along the road, some youths came out of the town, and jeered at him, 'Go on up, you baldhead!' they said. 'Go on up, you baldhead!" (2 Kings 2:23, 9th century B.C.)

HOW THINGS HAVE CHANGED

The type of discipline problem youth leaders have today is much more serious than even a few decades ago. On the CBS evening news Dan Rather reported these alarming differences between discipline problems in schools in the 1940s and in the 1990s:

1940s	1990s
Talking	Drug abuse
Chewing gum	Alcohol abuse
Making noise	Pregnancy
Running in halls	Suicide
Cutting in line	Rape
Dress code	Robbery
Littering	Assault

The Rev. Jesse Jackson visited a Los Angeles high school and noticed the violence, vandalism, drug abuse, and students' empty, foggy minds. He recalled making the following comments in the principal's office after she told him how wonderful her students were: "I told her they were little gangsters. That her students weren't wonderful, but that they could be. We've got to change them. Our challenge is to make flowers bloom in the desert!"[4]

According to the Gallup polls of attitudes about education, lack of discipline in the schools has been rated the number one concern every year but one since 1969. No wonder—in junior and senior high schools across the country, homeroom teachers confiscate a literal arsenal of knives, brass knuckles, and guns. Boys are not the only ones guilty of aggressive behavior—teenage girls fight, spit at, and assault their teachers in a violent fashion. On the streets of Los Angeles and New York some girls carry small guns in their purses and razor blades in their mouths in case they need to protect themselves, or find a victim ripe for the taking. A third grade New Orleans girl recently took a .357-magnum to school to protect herself from a boy who was allegedly harassing her. Add to this the disciplinary problems surrounding teenage drug-use and the older, more familiar scenes of harassing teachers by walking in late, cursing, sleeping through class, and simple clowning around, and you begin to understand the pervasiveness of the problem. And if you think this description applies only to inner city schools, think again. Even parochial and affluent suburban schools are sorely afflicted with discipline problems.

In February 1993, Margaret Ensley's seventeen-year-old son Michael caught a bullet in the hallway of his high school in Reseda, Calif. She says a teen shot her son because he thought Michael gave him a funny look. Law enforcement and public health officials describe a virtual epidemic of youth violence in the last five years, spreading from the inner cities to the suburbs. "We're talking about younger and younger kids committing more and more serious crimes," says Indianapolis prosecuting attorney Jeff Modsett. "Violence is becoming a way of life." The widespread availability of guns is spreading. A

Harvard School of Public Health survey released in December of 1993 stated that 59 percent of children in the sixth through twelfth grades said "they could get a handgun if they wanted one."

In April, 1994, a Florida mall banned unsupervised teens from the premises before 6 P.M. on school days. Kim Blue, of Mall Owner Equity Properties, said, "There have been too many incidents of rowdiness, shootings, and stabbings." Between 1987 and 1991, the last years for which statistics are available, the number of teenagers arrested for murder around the country increased by an astounding 85 percent, according to the Department of Justice. In 1991, children from the ages of ten to seventeen accounted for 17 percent of all violent crime arrests. Teenagers are not just the perpetrators, they are also the victims. According to the FBI, more than 2,200 murder victims in 1991 were under eighteen, an average of more than six young people killed every day. An estimated 100,000 students carry a gun to school, according to the National Education Association. The Justice Department estimates that each year, nearly 1 million young people between the ages of twelve and nineteen are raped, robbed, or assaulted—often by their peers.

The National Center for School Safety reports that one in seven kids is a bully or a bully's victim. U.S. safety researchers believe 4.8 million kids fifteen and younger could be affected. Crimes range from stolen lunch money to bathroom beatings. Those who are victims of bullies suffer fear and shame. Some even drop out of school, run away, or commit suicide.

A history teacher with thirteen years of experience who recently retired to become an insurance agent shares these comments: "I chose teaching as a career because I loved the thrill of getting through to students, helping excite them about the world of ideas. But after being assaulted three times in the last two years and realizing my role was really that of a zookeeper, I decided to call it quits."[5]

One of the saddest commentaries comes from John Taylor Gatto, who was the New York State Teacher of the Year in 1991: "I've come slowly to understand what it is I really teach: a curriculum of confusion, class position, arbitrary justice, vulgarity, rudeness, disrespect for privacy. I teach how to fit into a world I don't want to live in."

Dr. Howard Hendricks in *Heaven Help the Home* puts it this way:

> We are living in a generation in which everything nailed down is coming loose. The things that people once said could not happen *are* happening. And thoughtful, though often unregenerate, individuals are asking, "Where is the glue with which to reassemble the disintegrating and disarrayed parts?[6]

Some frantic parents have put it bluntly: "You ought to bury them at twelve and dig them up at eighteen." Mark Twain said concisely, "When a child reaches twelve, we should put him in a barrel with a small hole in the side to feed him. Then when he reaches sixteen, we should plug up the hole." Unfortunately, this captures the sentiments of many youth workers as well.

WHAT TICKS YOU OFF

What ticks you off? What action do kids take that just gets under your skin? What is it that drives you up the wall? What is the activity that kids participate in that pushes all your wrong buttons? I've asked thousands of youth workers across the country those very questions. I've listed below many of their answers. Hopefully, the list will be an encouragement to you in helping you realize that you are not alone in your feelings of frustration, and that your youth group is fairly typical of many around the country.

- Bickering among group members
- Apathy
- Waiting to be entertained
- Lack of commitment or not taking God seriously
- Lack of respect for adults or others
- Arrogance
- Self-centeredness, cliques
- Unwillingness to listen
- Disrespect for rules and authority
- Complaining, negative attitude
- Lying
- Vandalism
- Put downs
- Acting too cool
- Know-it-alls
- Not listening
- Not cleaning up after a mess
- Horseplay
- Stubbornness
- Talking when someone else is talking
- Rudeness
- Belches
- Listening constantly to Walkmans and portable CD players
- Kids pushing the limit
- Coming to meetings late
- Spilling food and stomping it into the carpet
- Spitting
- Expressions made in a whiny voice, such as:
    "who cares"
    "stupid"
    "I'm not doing that"
    "I didn't know"
    "my father's an elder, board member, council member, etc."
    "all my friends do/don't"
    "make me"

"To keep junior highers from swinging from the balcony."

WHERE YOU FIT IN

Youth workers can help provide the "glue" of loving discipline that is lacking in the lives of many young people today. Which of the following disciplinarians best describes you?

• **Buddy—Permissive.** Buddy avoids absolutes and places no demands on his kids. His philosophy is that kids are basically good, and he refuses to be negative with them. He likes to let group members find their own way and feels his role is not to control or correct, but to support and encourage.

• **Ben—Benevolent.** Ben shows deep respect for and sensitivity to each individual in his group. He feels discipline is for the good of the students, not himself. He looks for long-range results and not temporary solutions. He remains aware of his own sinfulness and shortcomings.

• **Rocky—Authoritarian.** Rocky believes he has the final word in all disputes. His authority cannot be questioned. He places unrealistic demands on students and makes no allowances or exceptions. He feels his duty is to control, and he is not above using sarcasm and put-downs. He sees fear and pain as the best way to achieve discipline results.

Draw an "X" on the spot on the continuum where you think you are now:

Permissive————Benevolent————Authoritarian

Where would you like to be? Naturally Ben the Benevolent sounds like the person whose discipline style is most closely modeled on Christ-like behavior. But if we're honest, most of us have to admit to swinging, at times, toward one end of the line or the other. Sometimes we even jump from one extreme to the other. The good news is that you can change your style of discipline and turn it into an effective ministry tool—one that might just save your sanity!

NOW ASK YOURSELF

1. What is the difference between positive discipline and negative discipline?

2. Think of the discipline problems that were prevalent in your teen years and contrast them with the discipline problems faced by teachers and youth leaders today. What are the similarities and differences?

3. What types of discipline problems are in your city at home/school/church?

4. How are we doing in the above three areas in regard to discipline, and why?

5. What were your feelings when you read about the teacher with thirteen years teaching experience? Do you agree with his assessment? Why?

6. What are some of things kids do that tick you off?

THE GOAL IS MATURITY

Karen was the youth group "kiss-up." She was always polite and well-behaved in the youth group meeting when the youth sponsor was looking in her direction, but when the sponsor's back was turned, she could be a terror. She thought she was faking out all the authority figures in her life (parents, teachers, youth sponsors), but she wasn't. Confronting Karen with her rude and obnoxious behavior was difficult since she hid it from adults. Karen's life was always in turmoil. She had to be the center of attention in every activity, and her emotions were extremely volatile—either incredibly happy or in the pits. She always had a dramatic story to tell that could not wait.

Karen's values were not changed by her involvement in the church youth group; there she only learned how to fine-tune and perfect her hypocrisy. She never learned how to comfortably be herself and take responsibility for her own behavior. To those who first met her, she was a wonderful example of what a Christian environment can do for a young person's life, but to those who really knew her she was merely a demonstration of how easy it is for a young person to go through the outward motions of being a Christian without internalizing those values.

Karen's biggest problem was that she never developed self-control. The ultimate goal of all discipline: to bring kids to maturity and encourage self-discipline. Our objective is to prepare young people to make their own decisions in life and discipline themselves. We want to prepare each young person to become a fully functioning, mature adult. Discipline has been defined as *training that develops inner self-control in which values are internalized*. Discipline should help the teenager to establish a set of sound values and principles that he can use to conduct his life when his youth workers are not looking over his shoulder.

It may be possible to brainwash a young person to do anything you say, but who wants a youth group member who is merely going through some robotic motions? Such a student will not grow up and make her own decisions in life. The major emphasis must be on getting students to grow, mature, and learn responsibility for their own behavior. Simply designing consequences for misbehavior will not produce self-disciplined young people. Instead, use the strategies suggested in this book to increase student responsibility and self-discipline. Then the time spent with your young people will be an enjoyable time to look forward to, not anguish over.

Simply because a young person is compliant doesn't mean you have succeeded. Compliance means changing behavior in the presence of authority and only in the presence of authority. In street language, telling us what we want to hear is called "cheesing." A cheese ball is mostly air—it's not the real thing.

It's not too difficult to get young people to give the appearance of respect through bribery, force, cleverness, and peer pressure. But inside they may have problems you have no knowledge of because you've only controlled their outward actions. It reminds me of the mother who kept asking her five-year-old daughter to sit down. After asking repeatedly, the frustrated mother put the girl in the chair and vowed, "You will sit down!" The little girl merely smiled. When the mother asked her child why she was smiling, she replied, "I may be sitting down on the outside, but inside I'm standing up." Simply getting young people to go through the motions of obedience is not accomplishing the long-range goals.

I remember hearing about an elephant in a small traveling circus. The owner of the elephant would ask local residents of each town to give him $5 for the chance to try to get his elephant to jump off the ground with all four feet. If they succeeded they would receive $500. Many people tried using several methods to no avail. They tried to scare the elephant into jumping. However, this was a tired old elephant who was somewhat bored with all their efforts. Once in a while someone would get the elephant to lift one leg off the ground. The owner of the elephant was making a lot of money. Then one day a farmer came along and paid his $5. He stood in front of the elephant with two bricks in his hand. The elephant watched with curiosity as the farmer went to the back of the elephant. Then the elephant got the surprise of its life as the farmer smashed the two bricks together with the elephant's tail in the middle. The elephant jumped off the ground with all four legs and the man got his $500.

The owner of the elephant knew he had to change the contest, so in the next town he asked people to pay $5 to try to get his elephant to shake its head up and down and then right to left. If they could do it the owner would pay them $500. Many people tried to get the elephant to follow their hands as they waved them up and down in front of the elephant, but this elephant was either too wise, too tired, or again just plain bored, because it would just stand there chewing. A couple of days later the same farmer from the other town came and paid another $5. The farmer stood in front of the elephant holding the same two bricks and asked the elephant, "Do you remember me?" The elephant nodded its head up and down. Then the farmer asked, "Do you want me to do it again?" The elephant shook its head from right to left, and the farmer collected his second $500.

Several years ago I went to Sea World in San Diego and saw a small amphitheater with a sign that said "Roller Skating Ducks." My curiosity was aroused, so I took a seat and sure enough, the music started and out came these little ducks with tiny roller skates taped to their tiny, webbed feet. They were roller skating to the music. Yet as I looked closely at those ducks, I could tell their hearts just were not in it.

We can do the same things with kids by getting them to do a variety of things, but on the inside nothing has changed and you can tell their hearts just aren't in it.

EXTERNAL MOTIVATION—THE PROBLEM

External, or extrinsic, motivation occurs when an outside force causes us to take action. Offers of rewards or punishment make the individual respond. The problem is that when the reward or threat is withdrawn, the person may not internalize the principles and become self-disciplined. The acid test is, what are your young people like when you aren't there? Your daily battle may be won, but not necessarily the war, if an authority figure is constantly needed to insure proper behavior.

Leonard Berkowitz, in *The Development of Motives and Values in the Child*, describes how these values are to be internalized in the young people we are working with.

> When he is very young, of course, the child must be controlled by direct parental action. The mother must prevent her child from touching the hot stove.... As he gets older, he learns that his parents want him to do certain things at certain times and not to do other things. He gets approval for carrying out the desired actions and some form of punishment if he departs from his parents' standards.... This type of self-control is, however, ultimately based on the anticipation of detection; the child carries out the desired action or avoids the prohibited behavior because he believes that the people who can reward or punish him will find out what he has done. It is not until he has truly internalized parental and societal moral standards that he will behave in a socially proper fashion solely because that is the "right" thing.[7]

Your young people need assistance in learning how to face the challenges and obligations of living. They must learn the art of self-control. They should be equipped with the personal strength needed to meet the demands imposed on them by their youth group, school, peer group, and later adult responsibilities.

What do we want your young people to be like when they grow up? Most of the parents and youth workers I've met agree that they want to "influence" their young people to become responsible, independent adults. They want them to be able to make mature decisions about their faith, work, marriage, and parenthood. They want them to be discriminating in their judgment of people and ideas, and to live fully with a sense of adventure, unafraid to explore the world (even the universe) around them. They want their young people to be flexible enough to accept change, courageous enough to meet new challenges, and loving and sensitive enough to care deeply about life and people. "Control" over a young person only lasts until the child is bigger than you are; "influence" over a young person can last your lifetime and the young person's lifetime.

Standards are internalized when young people are asked to think about how they would like things to be. Too often students only react to what their youth leaders tell them to do, rather than being helped to decide what they would like to do for themselves.

The word "discipline" comes from the same root as "disciple." With discipline you are making disciples of your young people. To be a disciple of tennis or running, a person has to alter behavior, watch her diet, and change her daily schedule in noticeable ways. To be a responsible member of a youth group requires the same attentiveness.

Discipline often gets bad press because it's misunderstood. Discipline is not chaining young people to their seats or putting them in iron cages. People think discipline is synonymous with punishment, but in the Bible that's not the intended meaning at all. Both in the Hebrew and the Greek the words we translate *discipline* actually mean "training" or "education." The root word "disciple" means "learner." So discipline involves instruction and training as well as correcting, and it is to be motivated by love and concern (Heb. 12).

Positive Discipline vs. Negative Discipline

The concept of negative discipline implies the idea of holding a shotgun to a young person's head to get him to behave properly. A negative disciplinarian threatens, frightens, snarls, growls, bristles, and becomes just plain nasty in order to persuade young people to behave. Even if this kind of external pressure gets immediate results, when the pressure lets up, so does the person's response. Negative discipline usually backfires.

The most commonly used "shotgun" is guilt, and using it to get your teen to do something is destructive. First of all, guilt is a tremendously difficult feeling to carry around inside. Second, even if your young person does something for you because she feels guilty, she will resent it; that resentment, coupled with feelings of guilt, can produce intense feelings of anger.

Negative discipline can destroy a young person's sense of being loved and wanted. It can leave him feeling insecure and worthless. Negative discipline implies getting even, retaliation, vengeance, and exacting a penalty. Of course, all these dangers are increased whenever negative discipline is cruel, unreasonably severe, or prolonged.

When negative discipline is effective, it may still be weak because it controls behavior by establishing an avoidance response. Its weakness lies in the fact that negative discipline alone fails to teach young people to be responsible, motivated, and cooperative. Improved behavior at the threat of negative discipline simply means in this situation that the cost of negative discipline outweighs the benefits of misbehaving. The young person may change the way she behaves, but not change the way she *wants* to behave.

You may have heard you can train fleas. If you take a coffee jar, unscrew the lid, throw the fleas down into the jar, and put the lid back on, for a few minutes you will hear a popping noise. The fleas will bounce from the bottom to the top, and their little bodies will crash against the lid for a few minutes. Then they will get wise and won't jump as high, jumping instead just beneath the lid. They only go this far because of the pain (after a while, hitting your head isn't much fun). After a few hours of this you can unscrew the lid to that coffee jar and the fleas won't jump out. They have the capacity and ability to do it—in fact, they can jump much higher than that. But something tells them if they jump too high there will be pain. It does not, however, change their desire to jump that high. In the same way, negative discipline may make a teenager behave the way you want him or her to, but the person's desire to misbehave will remain.

The problem is that negative discipline is effective only as long as the threat hangs over an individual's head. Negative discipline does not teach the long-term benefits of changing behavior. Whenever young people realize that the threat of negative discipline has been removed, they are likely to begin engaging in the inappropriate behavior again.

Exceeding the speed limit on the freeway demonstrates how ineffective negative discipline can be when a threat is removed. When police cars are visible, most people carefully stay within the speed limit. When it is unlikely that police are around, many people exceed the speed limit. These people are willing to take the chance that they might get caught. Negative discipline procedures make the youth worker a police officer in the youth group.

I have heard the misconception that young people respect teachers who are tough. This probably grows out of the fact that typically we remember respecting teachers who consistently gave out fairly severe punishments for misbehavior. It seems logical that our respect grew out of the teacher's ability to punish effectively.

However, we also remember teachers who punished students and were laughed at. Why is it that students cringe when one teacher sends a student out of class, and smirk when another teacher does the same thing? The critical difference is not the use of discipline, but the youth worker's ability to combine positive interaction with consistency, fairness, and high expectations. Consequences are taken seriously because they are imposed within the context of a positive environment. A less-respected youth worker may try to use the same discipline, but will use it inconsistently and too frequently to have any impact.

This story quoted in Mary Schramm's book, *Gifts of Grace*:

> Once a little boy went to school. It was quite a big school, but when the boy found he could go right to his room from the playground outside he was happy, and the school didn't seem quite so big anymore. One morning when the little boy had been in school for awhile, the teacher said, "Today we are going to make a picture."
>
> "Good," thought the little boy. He liked to make pictures. He could make lions and tigers and trains and boats. He took out his crayons and began to draw. But the teacher said, "Wait. It's not time to begin." And she waited until everyone looked ready. "Now," said the teacher, "we are going to make flowers."
>
> "Good," thought the little boy, and he began to make beautiful flowers with his orange and pink and blue crayons. But the teacher said, "Wait." She drew a picture on the blackboard. It was red with a green stem. "There, now you may begin."
>
> The little boy looked at the teacher's flower. He liked his better, but he did not say this. He just turned his paper over and made a flower like the teacher's. It was red with a green stem.
>
> On another day the teacher said, "Today we are going to make something with clay." "Good," thought the little boy. He could make all kinds of things with clay—snakes and snowmen and elephants and mice—and he began to pinch and pull his ball of clay. But again the teacher said, "Wait, I'll show you how." And she showed everyone how to make one deep dish. The little boy just rolled his clay in a round ball and made a dish like the teacher's. And pretty soon the little boy learned to wait and to watch and to make things just like the teacher's. And pretty soon he didn't make things of his own anymore.
>
> And then it happened that the little boy and his family moved to another city and the boy had to go to another school. On the very first day he

went to school the teacher said, "Today we are going to make a picture." "Good," thought the boy and he waited for the teacher to tell him what to do. But the teacher didn't say anything. She just walked around the room. When she came to the boy she said, "Don't you want to make a picture?"

"Yes," said the boy. "What are we going to make?"

"Well, I don't know until you make it," said the teacher.

"How should I make it?" said the boy.

"Why, any way you like!"

"And any color?"

"Any color," said the teacher. "If everyone made the same thing in the same color, how would I know who made what and which was which?"

"I don't know," said the boy, and he began to draw a flower. It was red with a green stem.

We are not to stifle the creativity that exists in every young person. Too many times we end up putting kids in a box and limiting what they can become, all in the name of conformity. Don't do this to your kids. They are far too precious in God's eyes for us to destroy that wonderful spontaneity and love of life.

Negative discipline is merely an attempt to curb undesirable behavior. Negative discipline in itself does not teach or motivate a young person toward more desirable behavior. It tells a young person what *not* to do—it doesn't tell him what *to* do. Consider our jails and prisons. If punishment worked as a system for teaching people better behavior, then when criminals were released from jail after several years of incarceration, they would be straight from then on. Are they? The evidence is otherwise. A fantastically high percentage are back in prison in a relatively short time.

Dr. Bruce Narramore, in his excellent book *Help, I'm a Parent*, differentiates between negative discipline and positive discipline in the chart which follows.[8]

	Negative Discipline	Positive Discipline
Outlook	Eye for an eye	Done *for* kid, not *to* kid
Purpose	To inflict penalty for an offense	To train for correction and maturity
Focus	Past misdeed behavior	Future correct deeds
Attitude	Hostility and frustration	Love and concern
Resulting emotion	Fear and guilt	Security

THE PURPOSE OF DISCIPLINE

Discipline may come through words, deeds, or circumstances, but the purpose is always to develop maturity. That should be our goal in administering discipline and the ultimate goal of youth ministry (Col. 1:28). Our task is to prepare, disciple, and train young people to serve God with their lives—to bring them to maturity in Christ. A mature young person knows herself, accepts herself, and controls herself.

Discipline is more an attitude and atmosphere than an action. It is a tool, not a weapon. It is an expression of love, not anger. Discipline in the true sense of the word is positive, encouraging, and even proof of love.

Gordon MacDonald in *Parents and Teenagers* shares his definition of discipline:

> To me, discipline is the deliberate creation of stress in a relationship with your children in order to help them grow and learn. Discipline is setting them to a task to exercise, strengthen, and help them mature. Discipline is forcing them to face painful questions that need to be wrestled with. What a coach takes a team through *before* a contest is discipline.[9]

TOO LITTLE DISCIPLINE OR TOO MUCH?

Some adults believe you should not teach young people self-control. They believe it's best to stand back and allow teenagers to find their own paths and make their own mistakes without firm guidance. I disagree with this type of thinking. Fair and reasonable discipline is like a wall providing protection and defining limits, and demonstrates care and concern. Teens interpret a lack of discipline as a sign that no one cares.

However, since young people feel the need to express their independence, hyper-control can really make things worse. Too many rules and get-tough leaders offend kids and run them off.

The hands-off, anything-goes approach is equally disruptive. A teacher who has this kind of laissez-faire approach loses kids. When some of the kids who are inactive are visited, you soon discover that they have stopped attending because the class was so wild. Not all kids care for the loud, obnoxious behavior of their peers. Chaos might be fun for a few minutes, but not forever. Kids want order for the security it gives them.

This hands-off style is probably the most common response, especially from youth workers who fear if they react any other way they'll lose the kids' friendship. But this approach rarely works, and it carries other negative attributes:

• It teaches kids that it's okay to talk when someone else is speaking. Their leader doesn't seem to notice or care about the disruptive noise from the group.

•It offends the kids who want to listen but can't because of the noise.

•It says: "This is competition. May the loudest or longest talker win."

If we want an environment that attracts kids and encourages good behavior, we have to fall somewhere between these two extremes. Kids need a comfortable environment free of excessive control, but some control must remain. What will create something close to the proper environment is our unconditional love for the kids.

While we are not called to be watchdogs, drill sergeants, or undercover cops, we are not called to roll over and play dead, either. We don't need to be authoritarian, but we do have to be authoritative. We can't be permissive, but we have to be sensitive to everyone's needs. Discipline will be much easier on this middle ground between harshness and leniency.

Discipline is like a fence; it needs to be firm and strong to do the job for which it was intended, but it also must be flexible in case something unexpected happens. Don't forget that some young people require more discipline than others; that's just the way teens are.

The effective youth worker could be compared to a good fence builder—one who needs to keep in mind the following do's and don'ts:

• Discipline in the youth group is keeping such an orderly maintenance of "fences," or boundaries, that youth group members know exactly where the boundaries are. As long as they stay within the defined boundaries, punishment is not necessary.

• Don't build the fence so far away from the house that the young people can do virtually anything they want and still be within boundaries.

• Don't build the fence so close to the house that there is no room for the youth group to breathe—so close that it stifles creativity. Trying to maintain that kind of fence requires almost constant vigilance and often leads to constant punishment.

• Fence boundaries should be appropriate for the age and temperament of your group members and must be redefined as young people mature.[10]

I don't know of a young person today who doesn't really want to know where the boundaries are. There is security in knowing the limits. What young people don't want is to have the boundaries hammered on their youth meeting room door like Luther's ninety-five theses. They don't want to hear the rules recited every morning when they awaken. But young people do want to know the rules and have them enforced.

Giving a young person complete freedom and license is recognized today for what it is—a grave mistake. It places too much responsibility on shoulders that are not yet ready to carry it. The weight of the responsibility can be crushing. Too much discipline does practically the same thing as too little discipline. Too much also gives the young person a feeling of failure. Again, the burden is too heavy to bear.

BIBLICAL REASONS FOR DISCIPLINE

The Bible speaks of an unruly generation which would eventually come:

> For people will love only themselves and their money; they will be proud and boastful, sneering at God, disobedient to their parents, ungrateful to them, and thoroughly bad. They will be hardheaded and never give in to others; they will be constant liars and troublemakers and will think nothing of immorality. They will be rough and cruel, and sneer at those who try to be good. They will betray their friends; they will be hotheaded, puffed up with pride, and prefer good times to worshiping God. They will go to church, yes, but they won't really believe anything they hear." (2 Tim. 3:2-5, TLB)

Scripture teaches that the parents' relationship with their child should be modeled after God's relationship with people. This can also be applied to the youth worker's relationship with his or her young people:

> "My son, do not make light of the Lord's discipline, and do not lose heart when He rebukes you because the Lord disciplines those He loves [notice that discipline and love work hand in hand] and He punishes everyone He accepts as a son." Endure hardship as discipline; God is treating you as sons. For what son is not disciplined by his father? If you are not disciplined (and everyone undergoes discipline), then you are illegitimate children and not true sons. Moreover, we have all had human fathers who disciplined us and we respected them for it. [Notice the relationship between discipline and respect was recognized more than 2,000 years ago.]

No discipline seems pleasant at the time, but painful. Later on, however, it produces a harvest of righteousness and peace for those who have been trained by it (Heb. 12:5-9, 11).

Notice how God's fatherly love is characterized by tenderness and mercy. This love guides, corrects, and even brings some pain when it is necessary for eventual good. We would do well to follow this example.

A message youth workers especially can take to heart is again found in the book of Hebrews. "Therefore, strengthen your feeble arms and weak knees. 'Make level paths for your feet,' so that the lame may not be disabled, but rather healed" (Heb. 12:12-13). As much as you may be tempted to avoid the difficult job of discipline, strengthen your feeble arms and weak knees. The molding of young people into mature individuals is going to take work, and you'd better be prepared for it.

Paul offers us a warning on the subject of discipline: "Fathers, don't over-correct your children or make it difficult for them to obey the commandment. Bring them up with Christian teaching in Christian discipline" (Eph. 6:4, PH). How would a youth worker be guilty of overcorrecting or making it difficult to obey? By either over-disciplining or under-disciplining. Interestingly enough, both extremes produce the same result—insecurity.

There are other ways to—as the *King James Version* phrases it—"provoke young people to anger":

- compare or show favoritism
- accept conditionally
- embarrass or ridicule
- ignore
- be inconsistent
- show lack of sensitivity
- fail to forgive
- have too few rules
- overreact
- use sarcasm
- assign too difficult a task
- use put-downs
- condescend
- discipline in front of others
- accuse falsely
- be impatient
- interrupt
- use name-calling
- fail to respect privacy
- have too many rules
- punish unjustly
- shout or yell

A good reminder for all of us in youth work is, "Love forgets mistakes; nagging about them parts the best of friends" (Prov. 17:9, TLB). We need to be persistent but avoid the temptation to nag our students. Nagging has been defined as telling a person to do something when you know he hasn't forgotten. It has also been correctly described as being inefficient in the effort to promote desired behavior. Nagging is as widespread as the common cold. "Don't talk so much. You keep putting your foot in your mouth. Be sensible and turn off the flow!" (Prov. 10:19, TLB)

Many other verses in Scripture indicate the need for discipline in the lives of our children (as well as your youth group members). They include the following:

Folly is bound up in the heart of a child, but the rod of discipline will drive it far from him (Prov. 22:15).

Do not withhold discipline from a child; if you punish him with the rod, he will not die. Punish him with the rod and save his soul from death (Prov. 23:13-14).

He who spares the rod hates his son, but he who loves him is careful to discipline him (Prov. 13:24).

The rod of correction imparts wisdom, but a child left to itself disgraces his mother (Prov 29:15).

Discipline your son, and he will give you peace; he will bring delight to your soul (Prov. 29:17).

It is good for a man to bear the yoke while he is young (Lam. 3:27).

Discipline your son, for in that there is hope; do not be a willing party to his death (Prov. 19:18).

[The Lord said to Samuel about Eli:] "For I told him that I would judge his family forever because of the sin he knew about; his sons made themselves contemptible, and he failed to restrain them (1 Sam. 3:13).

From Genesis to Revelation, there is a consistent foundation on which to build an effective philosophy of discipline in youth work in order to bring young people to maturity in Christ. When we depart from the standard which is clearly outlined in the Old and New Testaments, we pay a high price in the form of lost ministry opportunities and high youth- worker turnover. Self-control, human kindness, and respect can be part of our youth groups if we will discipline our young people out of, and with, love.

NOW ASK YOURSELF

1. What are you doing in the area of discipline? Are your methods causing inner changes of behavior/values or just outward appearances of responsible behavior?

2. Describe what you want your young people to be like after they leave your youth group.

3. If discipline is like a fence, what kind of fence are you using? When is it too close (restrictive) or too far removed?

A. Picket	F. Electric fence
B. Chain link	G. Portable fence
C. Barbed wire	H. Door
D. Brick wall	I. Net
E. Moat	

4. Do you think 2 Timothy 3:2-5 describes today's generation? Why or why not?

5. Describe the kind of discipline God uses with us.

6. Think of areas in your ministry where you have "provoked a young person to anger." Has this been cleared up?

7. How do you feel about taking verses directed to parents and applying them to youth leaders? Is there a fine line or danger in doing this? Are some youth workers trying to take the place of parents?

*"Then it's agreed. The theme for this year's youth convention is
'Hey, Gang! Let's Not Trash the Hotel!'"*

REASONS FOR PROBLEM BEHAVIOR

The next time you have close friends over for dinner or conversation, try playing the "remember when" game. Share some of what you are doing with your young people and then ask your friends to remember when they were adolescents. Do they remember someone making a remark about how they looked (the shape of his head, the size of her nose)? How did such remarks affect them? You will be amazed at how much good information you can obtain that will help you recognize how sensitive teenagers are to criticism and rejection. They want to be accepted and liked, just as you did.

Not long ago, several of us played the "remember when" game after an enjoyable but intense game of Monopoly. Sitting back in a comfortable easy chair, Sharon remembered a name she was called in junior high. She had a bright-red birthmark on her upper lip, and the other kids called her "dog face" or would yell things like, "Here doggy, here doggy." She described how extremely difficult it was for her to cope—so difficult that she had contemplated suicide. Mark said he tended to be extremely shy in his teen years and could remember his mother answering any question directed at him before he could get an answer out. John remembered never wanting to take a shower in junior high physical education class. He recalled how most of the students would just run through the showers and grab a towel.

I can remember the fear that gripped me soon after my junior year in high school just after I had become a Christian. We had a prayer circle in our church youth group with everyone holding hands and praying in turn. I had never prayed in public, and as it got closer to my turn, I was so nervous I started to perspire and shake. When it came my turn I said something quickly (I had no idea what I prayed) and the prayer time moved on to the next person. To this day I remember my fear of being embarrassed in front of my peers.

I recently read a newspaper story about a boy in a small high school who was overweight. Everyone made fun of him. They would call him "blimp" or "fatso" or "lard." He was the butt of every joke. He was a nice kid and never gave his teachers any trouble, but one day he had finally had it. He brought a gun to school and shot several of the students, finally turning the gun on himself. His suicide note explained that he could not endure the ridicule any longer.

How often we forget or minimize the intense trials and tribulations many young people go through during junior high and high school. We almost have a protective amnesia that blocks out our worst memories of that age. In addition to playing the "remember when" game, your memory will be helped if you invite a Christian doctor who deals with adolescents to talk to you and your youth work team. It is important to find a doctor who really knows about this period of human development and who wants to share that knowledge with others. Understanding the physical changes teenagers are going through will help you understand their behavior and extreme mood swings.

"Will it not be a glorious day when adults generally look upon bothersome young people as individuals who are trying to *solve* problems instead of individuals who are trying to *be* problems?"[11] These words of the late child psychiatrist J. S. Plant are worth thinking about. If you can learn to hunt for the cause of a young person's misbehavior and help her solve her problem, you can save her and yourself a great deal of pain and anxiety. A few minutes given to prevention are worth hours of psychiatry.

EMOTIONAL ROLLER COASTERS

Most of us can vaguely remember—with some difficulty—what it was like to leave childhood behind and become adolescents. Our minds tend to repress those early years when some of life's most painful experiences occurred. Remember the embarrassment and humiliation of struggling with parents for independence, times of rejection by the peer group, guilt feelings brought on by a new awareness of sexuality, love triangles, and broken hearts. These are some of the difficulties adolescents face.

Emotionally, young people are on a roller coaster. It's either Death Valley or Mount Everest. At youth group meetings they're great one week and a disaster the next. It's incredible! One week students are listening intently, participating, well-behaved, and asking terrific questions. You go out of the youth meeting riding on a cloud, life is tremendous, you love kids. But the next week it's disaster city. You wonder if they went home the week before and called each other, saying, "Hey, we were too nice last week." It's important during those trying times that you not blame yourself or take it personally. There is a tendency to think you are not getting through or that your teaching has gone in one ear and out the other. It can be horribly frustrating. But be assured that the time you've spent on your young people hasn't gone to waste; it will pay off. You can bank on it.

What we remember most about being adolescents is that no one understood us and that we worried a lot about ourselves. We worried that we were growing too rapidly, too slowly, too unevenly—or developing too much, too little, or in the wrong places. We worried about our size, about being overweight, about having a skin condition, about lacking muscular strength, or about underdeveloped physical characteristics (i.e., breasts or genitalia). It seemed as though parts of our body were in a conspiracy against us. We didn't understand ourselves well, and neither did our parents or teachers.

The emotional world of the teen is typically fast and intense. Remember that adolescence is a period of transition. A prevailing characteristic of change is *instability*. When something is going through a transition, it is less structured internally. A less powerful stimulus will trigger a more intense reaction.

Dr. G. Keith Olson describes these emotions that are experienced over a brief period of time in one teen's life:

> 6:30 A.M.—Jennifer wakes up reluctantly, dreading this day which she is absolutely positive will be awful.
>
> 6:50 A.M.—She is elated because she can still fit into her favorite pair of pants.
>
> 7:00 A.M.—She is upset because her hair will not do what she wants it to do. She knows she will feel humiliated when the other kids see her.
>
> 7:30 A.M.—She is both thrilled and apprehensive because Jeff called, asking to drive her to school that day.
>
> 7:50 A.M.—Pride, even arrogance, is what Jennifer feels as her friends see her driving into the school parking lot, snuggled close to Jeff.
>
> 7:55 A.M.—She feels indignant and angry as she sees her friends walk off to class ahead of her after making a snippy remark about her special transportation.

In just ninety minutes Jennifer experienced intense feelings of reluctance, dread, elation, humiliation, thrill, apprehension, pride, arrogance, indignation, and anger. Girls are especially prone to experience intense emotional reactions because of cultural and social influences that encourage girls to express their feelings. Cultural influences discourage emotional expression in boys.[12]

It doesn't take a psychiatrist to understand why young people sometimes behave like smart alecks. One of the main reasons is confusion; the young person is finding his place in society and discovering who he is. Attempting to show his maturity, he tests those in authority while portraying a superior and confident attitude (which adults see as being cocky and smart-alecky).

Romantic problems can definitely affect a teen's life. The girl whose boyfriend dumped her, or the boy who was turned down one too many times by the girl of his dreams is likely to be moody and depressed, show no interest in church or youth group, and be obsessed with thoughts of lost opportunities for romance.

But what is this problem which so many adolescents face at this time of life? What is it that causes so much hurt and pain in young people between twelve and twenty years of age? It's a feeling of hopelessness that we call "inferiority." It's that awful awareness that nobody likes you; that you're not as good as other people; that you're a failure, a loser, a personal disaster; that you're ugly, or unintelligent, or don't have as much ability as someone else. It's that depressing feeling of worthlessness.

Teenage boys especially tend to strike out physically at others when they feel powerless to get their way by other means. These young people often lack verbal skills and believe in a distorted version of the actions-speak-louder-than-words model of living.

In today's youth culture, there are no absolutes. Young people are bombarded with the idea that there is no right or wrong. This piles confusion on confusion, as nothing in life seems secure for a teen.

The disappearance of marriage as a dependable, permanent structure has caused many changes in families. Parents are going through their own midlife crises. Self-absorbed with their own problems (divorce, job changes, unfulfilled goals), they cannot protect, guide, or support their teenagers.

Families are smaller, and those smaller families are more mobile (20 percent of the population moves every year). The kids in smaller families tend to be more self-centered because parents are able to cater to the individual needs of their kids.

Sometimes deficiencies in our youth groups lead to troublesome behavior. In many cases, there are simply no payoffs for following the rules. Boredom is often a major problem because the curriculum is not up-to-date, or youth leaders are so overworked they have little time for innovation or creativity. Poorly kept physical facilities and inadequate recreational facilities also contribute to disciplinary dilemmas.

Kids who grow up in families where there is child abuse and maltreatment, spouse abuse, and a history of violent behavior learn early on to lash out physically when they are frustrated or upset.

Poverty exacerbates the situation. Parents who haven't finished high school, who are unemployed or on welfare, or who began their families when they were teenagers are more likely to have delinquent teens.

STRESSED-OUT KIDS

Thousands of kids are like pressure cookers. And while most teenagers seem to handle pressure fairly well, youth workers need to know the causes of stress and how to help teenagers deal with it. Lots of "under-pressure" kids need your support. And you can make a difference. The stress teenagers face frequently mirrors adult stress. School concerns are similar to job concerns. *Psychology Today* reported that receiving failing grades in school or breaking up with a boyfriend or girlfriend were stressful to teenagers.

Besides school concerns, teenagers face the same family concerns that adults face. *U.S. News and World Report* reported on a federal government study showing growing psychological stress on children. The study stated, "In the last fifteen years, 15.6 million marriages have ended in divorce, disrupting the lives of 16.3 million children under the age of eighteen."

Young people can't escape the problems of stress any more than adults can. All are under stress. The dilemma is knowing how to respond to stress in productive ways. For example, some kids go through a breakup of a relationship relatively unscathed, while others experience severe trauma over it. What makes the difference?

Kids who learn healthy coping skills and have supportive friends and family stand a better chance of surviving stress.

WHAT SHOULD WE DO?

Youth workers agree that no simple answers to these problems are available. But here are some ways to cope with misbehavior, and also some methods to avoid.

Since many young people make a game out of breaking rules to challenge authority, one logical starting point is to place responsibility for making and enforcing rules on the young people themselves. This approach uses peer pressure to maintain disciplinary order and has worked well in some settings. The major problem with this approach occurs when model students, who are not themselves disciplinary problems, are put in charge of this system; their troublemaking peers don't really feel pressure from people their own age.

To be helpful we need to respond genuinely to our young people's moods and feelings without being infected by them. We need to help our teenagers with their anger, fear, and confusion, without ourselves becoming angry, fearful, and confused. Be sensitive to their feelings.

The problem is that young people often don't know how they feel. They are experiencing feelings that are totally new to them, and they can't even begin to put these feelings into words. They are embarrassed and confused because they can't express their feelings. They don't understand their feelings, and they don't want to admit that to their youth workers, so they no longer confide in or share things with them. By spending time with students, drawing them out, and showing sensitivity to feelings—whether the feelings are expressed or not—you can build strong relationships with your young people and help them deal with these feelings.

Keep in mind that drastic, lightning-quick changes of feelings and moods are completely age-appropriate for teens. They are normal and natural teen behavior. While youth workers may find these abrupt changes irritating, exasperating, and difficult to cope with, it may help to realize that "this too shall pass."

Spiritual shifts are as common as emotional ones. Church youth groups are known for spiritual highs after summer retreat or returning from choir tour. Unfortunately, they are also well known for spiritual valleys between these special events. This characteristic cycle between mountaintop highs and valley lows is usually not so much a sign of unhealthy spirituality as a product of adolescent emotional changeability. Change is part of being a teenager—physically, emotionally, and spiritually.

As we deal with reasons for misbehavior among students, it's important to deal with teens on their level and not widen the gap between us that already exists because of age difference. A mistake adults often make is to say, "When I was your age. . . ." This phrase brings instant deafness to young people. They do not want to hear how good we were and how bad they are by comparison. Even if they hear us, they do not believe that we were as hard working, sensible, smart, thrifty, and well-behaved as we say. In fact, sometimes they have difficulty imagining that we were *ever* young. Comparing ourselves to them—and making ourselves look better—will not encourage kids or help them become closer to us. Show you understand their feelings and that you care—without the "When-I-was-your-age" speech.

It's easy to lose touch with what's going on with young people. So ask kids what kinds of pressure they have, and then listen to what they say. The key word is "listen." Simply being attentive and offering compassionate responses and ideas can help alleviate some of the teenagers' pressures. Provide a safe environment for your group members to talk about their pressures by being available, listening instead of lecturing, and offering suggestions for healthy ways to deal with stress.

You can give your teenagers concrete ways to deal with their stress. If you give them this gift, you won't take away the potential pain and hurt that life sometimes brings—but you'll teach teenagers positive ways to cope.

PEER PRESSURE

The peer structure in your youth group has important effects on friendship patterns. These patterns, in turn, have important effects on the social behavior and achievement of the young people. The degree to which a young person is liked or disliked by others in the youth group will help shape how she feels about herself. The social position of the young person in relation to others has a direct bearing on her attitudes toward herself and toward the youth group. Furthermore, her own evaluation of her relative position in the peer group structure often determines how the student will use her ability in the youth group. Someone who sees herself as well-liked will tend to express more positive feelings toward self, others, and the youth group. The young person who sees herself as disliked tends to express more negative feelings.

Social life can make or break a teen's self-esteem. All the adulation and love in the world from one's parents and youth leaders may not mean as much as acceptance by one's peers. Being a social outcast can seriously influence a teen's performance in youth group. Teens who don't fit in may appear lazy, bored, or uninterested because they are wrapped up in the problems of their social lives.

Beth, a member of our youth group, appeared to everyone as aloof and reserved. She attended almost every youth group activity, but she always seemed to cling to the youth workers' sides. She often preferred helping the adult youth workers instead of participating in an activity with her peers. To help get Beth more involved with peers, one of the youth leaders casually suggested to some of the other teens—who were talking about going to the movies that weekend—that they invite several other kids, including Beth. They did ask her along, and that was the turning point for Beth. She began to emerge from her shell and was able to feel far more comfortable with the youth group once she knew she was accepted. All it took was a little nudging on the part of a concerned youth worker.

You see, when you feel worthless and foolish—when you don't like yourself—then you are more frightened by the threat of ridicule or rejection by your peers. You become more sensitive about being laughed at. You lack the confidence to be different. Your problems seem bad enough without making them worse by defying the wishes of the majority. So you dress the way they tell you to dress, you talk the way they tell you to talk, and all your ideas are the group's ideas. All these behaviors have one thing in common: they result from feelings of inferiority.

Young people who can't fit in with one social group may choose another group to hang out with but may never really be comfortable there. They may seem to have perpetual chips on their shoulders and may bad-mouth the group they really want to be accepted by. They are often very negative in their outlooks about school and church because of this.

POSITIVE PEER PRESSURE

Peer pressure doesn't have to be negative. We are all aware of how youth group members encourage and reinforce a problem student's disruptive behavior. This negative peer pressure is often a major contribution to problem behavior. But the same peer pressure with a positive direction can be a great tool in getting problem young people to "clean up their acts" and improve their behavior.

Positive peer pressure works this way: enlist the aid of key group members, choosing those with emotional and spiritual maturity. Encourage these leaders to exert their influence for the good of group members and the group as a whole.

One example of how positive peer pressure worked in our group involves a student we'll call Bill. Bill wasn't a bad kid, but he was always getting into some minor trouble. When we went to Tijuana to distribute food and clothing, he would buy fireworks to sneak back across the border. In Sunday School, when it was time to break into small discussion groups, he would always be the last one to drag himself into his group or he would explain how he could participate from outside the circle and didn't need to move. A variety of methods were used to try to get Bill involved, but the one that worked was simply having some of the kids say positive things about him when he did participate. He would then get this little grin on his face, a somewhat surprised "I-did-good" look. Bill started to share more in the discussions, even to the point of volunteering to take the lead one week.

•**Form small peer-support groups.** Have kids meet in cluster groups of no more than five to discuss kids' problems, brainstorm solutions, and pray for each other. Peer support groups provide an opportunity for you to get to know kids on an intimate level. The groups also provide a place for young people to "let their hair down."

•**Provide peer counselor training.** Use Barbara Varenhorst's peer-counseling model to give young people listening skills, questioning skills, ways to negotiate with adults and ways to help each other. Barbara's program provides tools for kids working with other kids and teaches kids interpersonal skills for communicating with their parents, teachers and peers. For peer-counseling information, write to Barbara Varenhorst, Director, Palo Alto Peer Counseling Program, 25 Churchill Ave., Palo Alto, CA 94306.

THE NEED FOR ATTENTION

If we tell a young person often enough that he is bad or stupid or evil, he may believe us and adjust his behavior accordingly. In fact, if he receives more attention from acting in a destructive way than from being well-behaved, why should he want to conform? Attention gained in any manner is better than no attention at all. One of the main reasons for misbehavior is the need to gain attention.

Dr. Fitzhugh Dodson, in *How to Discipline with Love*, describes this concept using the law of the soggy potato chip. As it applies to youth work, the law goes like this: A young person prefers a fresh potato chip to a soggy one. But if the choice is between a soggy potato chip and no potato chip at all, he will settle for the soggy one. In the same way, a young person prefers his youth worker's positive attention to negative attention. But if the choice is between negative youth worker attention and no attention at all, the teenager will usually choose the negative attention. To a young person even negative attention is better than being ignored. [13]

A youth worker intends negative attention to be a form of discipline. But strangely enough, to a young person it may act as a reward. The result is that many youth workers are teaching their young people the exact opposite of what they really want them to learn.

Positive attention naturally falls to those who do well. On the other hand, negative attention naturally falls to those who have problems. The primary difference between motivated and turned-off students is not the need for attention, but the way they have learned to get attention. Because students will get attention one way or another, give them the kind that is helpful—praise for doing the right things (discussed in chapter 4).

NOW ASK YOURSELF

1. Play the "remember when" game. Describe your life during your teen years, specifically in the areas of emotions/feelings.

2. What worried you most in your teen years? What would you identify as the top concerns of the young people under your care and guidance today?

3. In what group(s) were you as a teen?

A. Athletics	I. Surfer
B. Drama	J. Cowboy
C. Journalism	K. Drug/alcohol
D. Music	L. Too cool/popular
E. Intellectual	M. Heavy Metal
F. Band	N. Skater
G. Minority	O. Wallflower
H. Cheerleader	Other:_____

4. How many young people in your youth group come from single-parent families? How does this affect your youth group? What is your church doing to minister to these families?

5. Why should a young person behave in your youth group?

6. How do you respond genuinely to your young people's moods and feelings without being infected by them?

7. Describe some of the emotions/feelings you have seen in your young people this last week.

8. Are there young people in your youth group who do not feel wanted? What can be done to help them?

9. What does a young person have to do to get your attention?

"OK, OK. We'll go to Disneyland."

GIVING KIDS CONFIDENCE TO BE ALL GOD WANTS THEM TO BE

Discipline should be enforced for our young people's benefit and not for ours. I have to be careful that I am not merely trying to create a showpiece. Do I care too much what others think about my kids and their reflection on me? All discipline and punishment should be done to help my young people be their best, not to make me look good or give me fewer problems. Imposing discipline for its own sake leads to a negative approach. Positive discipline places the emphasis on student needs and benefits.

We need to remain very positive and pleasant as we discipline kids. When I lose my temper, raise my voice, or put a kid down, I lose my credibility, build up barriers, and tear down a kid's self-esteem. In his book, *How To Really Love Your Teenager* (Victor, 1982), Dr. Ross Campbell said it this way:

> The more pleasant you are with your teenager, the firmer you can afford to be in setting limits and in discipline. Likewise, the more unpleasant you are with your teenager, the less firm you can afford to be. Why? First of all . . . the more unpleasant you are, the less your teenager will respect you and the more he will be inclined to go against your wishes. Second, the more unpleasant you are, the more parental authority you have dissipated in ventilating your anger and frustration. The more pleasant you are, the more parental authority you have saved to control your teenager's behavior.

THE ENEMY IS US

As the comic strip character Pogo said: "We have met the enemy and he is us." As youth workers we must accept personal responsibility for some of what goes on in our youth group. It helps to ask how much you are contributing to the discipline problems.

There is a story about a ship that was trying to make its way on a dark, foggy night, and all of a sudden saw in front of it a light. The captain flashed to the approaching ship, "Change your course ten degrees to the north." Within a few seconds a message came back to the captain, "Change your course ten degrees to the south." Well, that irritated the captain, so he sent out another message to this approaching ship. "I am a captain. Change your course ten degrees to the north." He got another message coming back.

"I'm a Seaman 3rd Class. Change your course ten degrees to the south." This infuriated the captain, so he sent out another message as they were coming head on. "I'm a battle-ship, change your course ten degrees to the north." He got another message back. "I'm a lighthouse, change your course ten degrees to the south."

I used to pray, "Lord, change my kids," and nothing happened. Then I began to pray, "Lord change me," and I began to see my kids in a different light. Sometimes we are the ones who need to move and change our own lives if we want to make a difference in the lives of kids.

Want to find out if you are a positive disciplinarian? You may find it helpful to ask a trusted coworker to observe your verbal and nonverbal behavior while teaching or leading a youth group meeting.

To help my adult volunteers in this area, I try to visit a different youth Sunday School class each week to observe classroom dynamics and the teaching styles of our teachers. I've discovered that we have some incredible volunteers who teach our young people. Each Tuesday at our teachers' meeting I have been able to pinpoint for them what they are doing that makes them so good. Each Tuesday I try to pick out one positive quality I observed the previous week. I might point out one teacher's ability to draw a response out of a quiet, shy young person; or the way another leader asks perceptive questions based on what was going on in the students' lives; or a certain teacher's insights into a particular passage. I will also bring up areas where teachers were a little weak as long as it is helpful to the entire group of teachers, and it will not embarrass them to do so publicly. I try to make it light and humorous. For instance, we had one teacher who had a habit of using the term "Father" repeatedly when leading in prayer. It got so that the kids in his class would keep count; one morning he used 26 "Fathers" in his prayer. I shared this one Tuesday and the teacher was surprised to learn he did this. Later he ex-plained how knowing about this habit helped him break it, and even joke about it with his class. So you see, a positive approach can work with volunteer staff as well as stu-dents.

ACCENT ON THE POSITIVE

To start building your positive disciplinarian skills, try this little exercise. For each youth activity imagine how your youth group would look if it were composed of only mature and cooperative young people. (Am I asking the impossible?) Picture your group com-posed of members who are motivated and responsible. Once you envision how you would like young people to participate in activities, you are on your way to teaching young peo-ple to meet your positive expectations.

Gordon MacDonald explains that there are two ways to paddle a canoe through white water. You can wait until you get into the rapids and then decide what you're going to do. But you'll probably end up falling into the water. Or you can keep your eyes fifty yards downstream, picking out your route so you know exactly how you're going to act before you get there. Most youth workers make their errors by failing to plan ahead and think about what kind of young people they hope to produce.

When I was younger, I was taught that if you have high expectations of young people, you'll always be disappointed. Not necessarily true—in fact, it often works just the opposite way. When others have high expectations of you, then there is more incentive to perform well. Warren Bennis in "The Unconscious Conspiracy: Why Leaders Can't Lead," finds ample reason to agree: "In a study of school teachers it turned out that when they held high expectations of their students, that alone was enough to cause an increase of 25 points in the students' IQ scores."[14]

It was Ralph Waldo Emerson who said, "Our chief want in life is someone who will make us do what we can."

One of the biographers of Gandhi said this about him: "He often changed human beings by regarding them not as what they were but as though they were what they wished to be."

Our job as youth workers is to give kids confidence that God is working in and through them. Remember these are ordinary kids in the hands of the extraordinary God. We need to communicate to young people that we have confidence in them.

Learn to avoid these and other negative words and phrases which tend to discourage young people:

- "Let me finish that for you."
- "You are too slow."
- "I'm ashamed of you."
- "There isn't any excuse for this."
- "Can't you do anything right?"
- "Did you mess that up again?"
- "When will you ever learn?"

It is unhelpful to ask a young person, "What's the matter with you? Why can't you sit still? What has suddenly gotten into you?" These are unanswerable questions. Even if he knew, he could not explain his conflicting emotions, urges, and desires.

POSITIVE FEEDBACK

Telling young people what they do right is more important than telling them what they do wrong. Tell a young person how much you see him or her maturing and you will see a face light up. Reflecting positive qualities to your young people is one of the strongest ways to build positive self-images in them. To affirm their positive character traits, look for the positive things they do as they work alongside others in the youth group and let them know what you see.

Positive character traits might include the following:

Cheerfulness	Honesty
Compassion	Humor
Courageousness	Kindness
Courtesy	Loyalty
Creativity	Organization
Decisiveness	Patience
Efficiency	Punctuality

Enthusiasm	Respect
Fair-mindedness	Self-discipline
Flexibility	Sincerity
Forgiving spirit	Sympathy
Friendliness	Wisdom
Generosity	Understanding

Some youth workers have the wrong motivation for being positive around their young people. They try to use positive feedback as a way to get close to their kids. It's wonderful to be close to your young people, but don't use positive feedback merely as a tool to make you look good. This is a big mistake. The goal of positive feedback is to get a student to take pride in his or her behavior. The praise should not simply imply that the youth leader is trying to be a "buddy" to the young person.

GREAT EXPECTATIONS

Some youth workers never expect their young people to obey and thus they are seldom disappointed.

But when you believe in your kids, they'll rise to your expectations. Don't stifle their desire to succeed by telling them they can't. Instead, let your positive attitude rub off on them; it will show in their performance.

It's odd how faultfinding can make a young person deaf. He learns to turn off the negative youth worker because he knows what type of comments he is going to hear. Faultfinding is self-defeating; when you have a legitimate criticism, the young person is not likely to heed it. He has heard too many picky statements which he knows were not valid. Faultfinding does not usually change a person's behavior on a long-term basis. It may sometimes achieve immediate results, but lasting results are rare.

HOW TO BECOME A POSITIVE DISCIPLINARIAN

If being a positive disciplinarian calls for a dramatic change in your style of leadership, try these approaches:

• If you are set in your ways about how things are done in your youth group, then try to become more flexible by providing alternatives that encourage independent thinking and recognize individual learning styles.

• If you are labeling some of your young people as lazy, dumb, stupid, bright, charming, etc., then try to stop and begin to see them as real people with both positive and negative qualities. Help them overcome the negative while building on the positive qualities.

• If you are given to blaming, ridiculing, teasing, or sarcasm, then try to stop it. No one likes this kind of behavior. They are put-downs that keep the war going.

• If you overreact to minor infractions of the rules, then try to count to ten before responding to the problem. Admit the problem to your young people. Talk about your feelings. Listen to theirs. Ask for help in creating and enforcing humane rules.

• If you are behaving like a traffic cop, then try to learn what to see and what not to see.

• If you are unwilling or unable to smile, or find humor in the daily turmoil of life with students, then you are in the wrong line of work. Humor and a quick, frequently used smile are the best tools a youth leader has for maintaining peace and sanity in the youth group.

QUALITIES OF A POSITIVE DISCIPLINARIAN

Some basic inner qualities are important in those who have authority over young people. As you study the following characteristics of a positive disciplinarian, try to identify areas needing improvement in your own life.

Practice What You Teach. Youth workers must set the example of how they want their group to behave. You are the blueprint for the kids you work with. "A student is not above his teacher, but everyone who is fully trained will be like his teacher" (Luke 6:40). Young people desperately need mature adult leadership models. What we do speaks much louder than what we say.

John Wooden, former UCLA basketball coach, is certainly an example of this. Every player who has served under him has made the same comment. Whatever Coach Wooden asked them to do, he always did himself. If the players had to be in the motel at a certain time, he was in the motel at that same time. There were no double standards with him. He practiced what he preached.

Honesty. When you blow it and make a mistake, don't cover up and make excuses. Don't be afraid to say, "I'm wrong." If you expect the same honesty from your kids, set the example yourself. This isn't always easy. Sometimes we are afraid of showing weakness and inadequacy that may make us appear less than leaders.

I found myself struggling with the need for honesty late one Sunday evening on the bus returning from a great group experience at the beach—complete with campfire, wonderful singing, and a powerful prayer time. On the way home the bus suddenly stopped. The driver was puzzled about why it had stopped and wouldn't start (though we found out later it was simply out of gas). The kids were being themselves—talking and laughing; they didn't care if they would be late getting home. Because he could not hear the engine turn over due to the noise on the bus, the driver asked them to be quiet. The few that heard his feeble appeal did get quiet, but the rest of the bus hadn't heard his request, so they kept talking and giggling.

At this point I got out of the church van and stepped into the bus. I was tired and wanted to get home and could only think of the sixty sets of parents waiting for us. I started yelling about how rude they were with all their noise. (You must understand I am not normally a yeller.) It got deadly quiet on the bus as I ranted and raved for about five minutes. I then stepped out of the bus and realized how I had overreacted to a minor situation. I got back on the bus (which was still deadly quiet with the kids in shock from my outburst) and apologized to them. As difficult as it was to admit I was wrong, the incident drew us closer because the kids knew that even the youth minister blows it occasionally (I'm positive they already knew this), but he's not afraid to admit it and ask forgiveness.

Wisdom. Pray for wisdom as a disciplinarian. A lot is left up to your judgment. Sometimes you are forced to make decisions quickly and there is a lot to think about:
- Who is responsible?
- What was the motive?
- Are they repentant?
- What kind of discipline is necessary?
- What are the circumstances?

My need for wisdom was glaringly apparent one evening when I walked into the youth building and heard the sound of breaking glass. I ran to the bathroom where the noise had come from, and discovered pieces of broken mirror scattered all over the floor. I also found a guilty-looking high schooler with skin torn from his knuckles. Sherlock Holmes fan that I am, I used some elementary deduction and concluded the young man had broken the mirror with his fist. (And you thought youth ministers were only good for volleyball.) This particular young person had a bad track record and was consistently getting in trouble. I was ready to pounce on him. Instead I sent up a quick prayer and began asking nonthreatening questions to find out what had happened. It turned out that this guy's girlfriend was going out with someone else. Instead of hitting the new boyfriend, he hit the mirror without meaning to break it.

I said very little. He knew what he did was wrong and he was sorry he had done it. We cleaned up the broken mirror together and he did extra jobs around the church the next month to pay for a new mirror. We became friends during that time and I was able to use the opportunity to share with him about the Lord. I'm still grateful for God's wisdom in handling a potentially volatile situation.

Patience. All youth leaders need an extra dose of patience. I'm not talking about ignoring the problem, but simply being under control yourself. Remember, these are kids. If they were perfect, then you wouldn't be needed. You would be out of a job.

Too often we are like the teacher who saw a student—who acted like he had rocket fuel in his body—messing around in class and asked, "Who made you?" The kid responded "God!" The teacher replied, "Well, He didn't do a good job." The student's comeback was, "That's because He isn't finished with me yet!"

Teenagers are not little adults. Many times they handle situations poorly. That's one of the reasons you are around—to guide and teach them the correct way to handle anger, frustration, bitterness, and exasperation. I'm not saying you have to be perfect in the area of patience, but let's hope that we are a little further along on this than the kids we are teaching.

Just as love can cover a multitude of sins, impatience can destroy months of ministry. It takes only one untimely outburst or overreaction and some young people will cross that youth worker off their lists for months. It's that hot-tempered outburst that I try to avoid.

Teamwork. The entire youth staff must reinforce and believe in the same rules; they must stand behind one another. If they don't, a young person soon learns who is the easiest to sway and who is the weakest link. If youth workers disagree about discipline in a particular situation, they need to get behind closed doors and say, "If we can't agree on discipline, let's at least agree that it's more important for the young people's welfare that we be united than it is for anyone's opinion to prevail."

One year we had an extremely rowdy group of hyperactive high school guys on a camping trip. They were in a tent with an inexperienced counselor (that was the first mistake). The campers in his tent explained how they wanted to scare the other campers in our group in this public campground. We had agreed as a team of counselors before the camp-out began that when it was time for lights out, we would keep all of our campers in their tents for the rest of the night. This particular counselor, however, decided that the best way to get his campers in his tent to like him was to let them be the only ones to run around "for only ten minutes" that night. His campers not only scared our campers but also other campers not a part of our group in this public campground. Then they got a little more daring and started pulling up tent pegs of campers not belonging to our group and throwing food around the camp. This went on for twenty-five minutes. The park ranger eventually quieted things down, but our reputation was shattered and our impact for the Lord was negative for the remainder of our time in the campground.

Young people need to see unity between their youth workers. There cannot be one youth worker openly dissenting. It's like a football team; it's better for everyone to execute the play the quarterback calls than for half the team to do one thing and half to do another.

Be loyal to those in authority over you. If the senior minister or church board makes a rule you don't like, talk to them privately. Don't debate the rightness or wrongness of these rules in front of your young people. Don't paint those in authority as the bad guys. Don't say, "They gave us this dumb rule. I hate it too, but we have to do it." You do neither the young person nor those in authority any good by off-the-record remarks. Discipline has to be a *team* effort.

Be Consistent. Consistency is the backbone of discipline. Inconsistent or contradictory discipline is more confusing and harmful to a young person than the extremes of too much or too little discipline. You will not find any form of discipline useful unless you are definite, firm, and consistent in what you ask and forbid.

Sometimes a warning acts as a challenge to a young person. He will do what you've warned him against just to see if you'll carry out your threat. He knows what the penalty will be and is ready to risk it, just like some students of mine who took the challenge of breaking camp rules one summer.

At summer camp the last night is always the most difficult as far as keeping kids in their cabins after lights out. The campers know they will be going home the next morning, so they figure there is not a lot the leaders of the camp can do to them. I had one group of guys in my cabin several years ago who were a lot of fun, though they were always getting into something. Maybe that's what made them so much fun. They were into everything and they were lively.

Unfortunately for these guys, I overheard their plan to get up in the middle of the night and do some raiding of the girls' cabins. That night, when they thought I was asleep, they began to wake each other up without making a sound. They were good at it! I could barely hear them whispering to each other as they dressed silently in the darkness of the cabin. It took all twelve of them about ten minutes in the dark to put on their warm clothes and tiptoe over to the cabin's only door.

When I heard the hand on the doorknob, I quietly but firmly cut through the darkness of the room with, "Everybody back in his bed now!" For the next two minutes (which seemed like forever) there was no movement, and I could tell it was a standoff. I could hear them whispering, figuring out the odds. Obviously twelve against one was not odds in favor of my physically stopping them. I could hear them questioning what I could and would do. I repeated my message one more time. Another long silence. Then one by one they went back to their beds. I knew they were disappointed that their plan was foiled, so I told them what a great plan it was and how they almost got me. We started talking about it and had a great laugh. They knew I was on their side, but they also knew I would be consistent even the last night of camp.

Mean what you say. Don't beg kids to behave. You cannot be wishy-washy if you want to be effective. Kids can spot hesitancy a mile away. If you are uncertain, they will be attracted to you as bees are to honey, and they will begin to work on you to wear you down.

You should, therefore, never threaten consequences that you don't intend to carry out. When you've issued a warning, be sure to see it through. Any inconsistency in this respect is a blow to good discipline.

Young people must know that you will respond consistently and unemotionally to misbehavior. Some young people have learned that what some youth leaders say and what they actually do may be two entirely different things. Given this, you can safely expect to be tested. Young people need to find out if you mean what you say. You must, therefore, be prepared to implement the consequences you have established. As young people realize you are going to be consistent, they will abandon this type of testing behavior.

Consistency means no exceptions, even for the chairman of the board's kid. It means being consistent when there are only five minutes left in the class time. If you aren't consistent with only five minutes left, next week they will start acting up with ten minutes left.

Values and moral standards cannot be taught without consistent discipline. Consistency is much more important than severity. Therefore, there is a need to be careful not to be a moody or unpredictable disciplinarian.

Responsibility: Allow Them to Fail. In the Parable of the Prodigal Son (Luke 15), the father, I'm quite sure, tried to reason with his son before the son took off with his share of the estate. But once he left, the father let him be responsible for his own welfare, even when things didn't turn out too well. The father didn't send any people to bring him back, any money, or any help of any kind. He simply let his son experience hunger, filth, and failure before he eventually came home. The youth worker who is too anxious to bail young people out of difficulty may be doing them a disservice by depriving them of the experience of failure.

The Word of the Lord to Ezekiel clearly says we are responsible for our own actions: "The soul who sins is the one who will die. The son will not share the guilt of the father, nor will the father share the guilt of the son. The righteousness of the righteous man will be credited to him, and the wickedness of the wicked will be charged against him" (Ezek. 18:20). Your young people will experience pain and suffering as a result of their sins; Scripture teaches that we are morally accountable as individuals. Let students learn from their mistakes, take responsibility for them, and mature in the process.

Challenge your kids to take risks, even if it means failure. There are constructive lessons to be learned from failure, and failure can spur people on to impressive accomplishments if they don't give up and stop trying. The Wright Brothers failed in many attempts to make a flying machine; Winston Churchill was widely regarded as a political failure in his early career; Willie Mays got only one hit in his first twenty-six major league at bats. As long as failure doesn't become a way of life, it's nothing to be ashamed of.

Know What to Overlook. Always remember we can choose our battles. We can decide what is most important and not fight all the windmills at once. As William James said, "The art of being wise is to know what to overlook." Try to be sensitive to individual needs and don't make a major deal out of minor infractions.

In the book *Growing Pains in the Classroom*, Frank Johns shares this adolescent memory:

> [My algebra] teacher was Brother Albertus—known for his quick temper and the occasional use of physical force on students. I either did not have time to study [one] day, or I was just trying to see if I could get away with something, so I copied the formula for the binomial expansion on a cheat sheet and planned to use it on the test.
>
> I remember the excitement as I sat in class and slipped out the cheat sheet, while Brother Albertus walked along the rows of desks. The combination of fear and excitement is still very close to me as I write this story. Then somehow he saw me cheating. I don't remember how it happened, or how I could have been so careless, but he caught me. Brother Albertus came up to the desk and I was really scared—scared of physical punishment, scared of embarrassment, and scared that my parents would find out. I was rooted to the desk, wondering what my fate would be, looking at him, unable to say a word. He moved my test paper to one side and looked at both the cheat sheet and the test paper, and then marked no credit with his pen for the one problem.
>
> Brother Albertus never mentioned the incident to me afterwards, never told anyone else, and gave no indications to the class that it had happened.
>
> Many times as a teacher, when I was in a position similar to that of Brother Albertus, I remembered this incident. I had "learned a lesson" in honesty without being humiliated or punished. The fact that the teacher knew and I knew what happened was punishment enough. Finally, I learned that if rules or laws, either in school or elsewhere in society, are broken, I have to deal with each case individually and not just "go by the book."[15]

Learn to Laugh. Don't take youth work too seriously. I know full well how exhausting youth work is, how it tests your mettle to the Nth degree, how important it is to be a good youth worker. But that doesn't mean you should never crack a smile. Young people can be hilarious! Sometimes you can be hilarious when you try to be an ogre and you find yourself way off base. Laugh at yourself. Laugh with your young people. Laughter can drown a multitude of sorrows and tensions so they don't turn into tears. The world has enough gloomy, frowning faces; bring a smile to your youth group and share it with your kids.

Sometimes you have to laugh with kids just so you don't kill them. For example, at an overnight retreat in a mountain cabin, Bob Merrill, minister of youth at a Presbyterian church in New Jersey, had a heart-stopping experience. In the evening the two genders departed to their respective rooms. When Bob woke up in the morning he felt an impending sense of aloneness. He found all the youth group sleeping in the living room of the cabin with no supervision. As he counted heads (or toes, depending on what was showing from under the sleeping bags), his eyes came to the middle of the floor. His heart grew faint as he saw *four* feet protruding from the end of an unzipped and folded-over sleeping bag. He could see the headlines: "Youth Minister Arrested after Retreat Orgy." As he was about to let them have it with both barrels, he rolled back the sleeping bag and found Tom and Sam grinning from ear to ear as they yelled, "Good morning, Bob. Got ya!" They got him and he knew it! He and the entire youth group had a great laugh.

Having a sense of humor not only means you can take a joke. It also means you can say, "All right—I made a mistake, but it didn't wipe me out." Young people need to know that failure isn't fatal—and they also need a Christian model who isn't always perfect.

Someone with a sense of humor isn't afraid to let his or her barriers down. You can become truly comfortable with him. He can relax around young people and enjoy being with them. He communicates to kids, verbally and nonverbally, that he likes them.

Being able to see humor even in difficult situations can ease tension and stress and get you through trying times. For the youth worker, a sense of humor is not an option—it's a prerequisite. Proverbs 17:22 says, "A cheerful heart is good medicine." Remember that youth workers need to be able to apply that medicine to the troubled spirits of today's young people.

Be careful how you use humor. If you tease, give a hard time, or say cruel things and disguise it as joking, don't be angry when your young people want to do the same thing to you. When a young person is interrupting a talk you are giving, the temptation is to come up with a clever line to embarrass him, such as: "John, you must have goat glands because you are always butting in," or "Laurie, it must take you twenty minutes to put your lipstick on because your mouth is so big." These lines can be cruel and demeaning. They model to the young person that "if you want to play cutthroat, I'm older and sharper than you are." Don't put a young person down and create a negative atmosphere. Don't nail him with derogatory remarks. Don't tear her down as a person.

Love Your Young People. Even in the ideal atmosphere, with the best programs, there can still be problem youth. When the rowdies surface, the first thing to do is try to develop a relationship with them. We can't effectively discipline someone we don't know. We have to earn the right to be heard, and we do that by spending time with them—visiting them in their homes or attending something they are a part of, like a band concert or a school play, a basketball game, or a debate tournament.

How do you help rowdies? The same way you help anyone—love them! Love them until you begin to understand them. Then love them some more until they know you have begun to understand them.

I have always been convinced that if you genuinely love young people, any form of discipline will work. A loving youth worker disciplines with a heart filled with compassion.

Unconditional love will help young people see themselves as significant and important to God. Look at every kid in your youth group as having potential, even the kid that drives you up the wall. Do you have that kind—the kind that you secretly pray will not show up at your next meeting, yet they come every week and sit in the front row? Remember, if a kid is sharp enough to get into trouble, he is probably creative enough to become significant. Don't focus on what a young person is, but on what he or she can become.

Never deprive a young person in any way that will make him feel unloved. Never say, "I don't love you when . . ." or "I won't love you if. . . ." Never use the "silent treatment," which only deprives the young person of your love and care for the time that you don't talk to him.

Perhaps you should spend some more time establishing the right youth worker/young person respect and love (mutually), and less time worrying about blind obedience. Mostly obedience comes out of love and respect for the person we obey.

A. W. Tozer once said, "God is not hard to live with." That helped me tremendously. God's standards and demands are high, but His resources are great. I want to be like that as a youth worker.

Love is still the greatest motive for obedience. We obey most whom we love most. And we love those who first love us (1 John 4:19). Love your young people unconditionally. Love your young people because you should love them, not because that's the way to get what you want. If your love is compelling, your young people will love you back. And unless there are competitive forces pulling harder than your love, they will obey, not because they must—but because they desire to.

In any youth group there must be affection, and a lot of it. Real, down-to-earth, sincere loving. The kind that carries conviction through touch, through the good mellow ring of the voice, through the fond look that says as clearly as words, "I love you for what you are beyond anything you might do. I love you because you are you." This kind of atmosphere can weather the storms of conflict that come up in every youth group.

Loving your kids includes knowing them and caring for them. Maybe the kid who is acting up has two parents who are constantly fighting and are considering a divorce. She may be living with a mother who is exhausted and trying to hold things together. She may sense rejection from her father. She may hear her parents yelling and screaming at each other over the phone each evening. She will not be wearing a sign as she enters your youth group that says, "Go easy on me today."

You must let your young people know that they are valuable to you. Character flaws and performance failure are two different things. There must be a love basis so that when a reprimand must take place it is not mistaken as a loss of love. You must also communicate that the performance is being reprimanded, not the character of the person. What a difference there is between saying, "You lied," and "You are a liar."

Closely linked with being loved should come the knowledge of belonging to some bigger whole. Our town, our school, our work, our family, our youth group—all bring the sense of togetherness, of being united with others, not isolated or alone. Create an atmosphere in your group that gives young people the security of belonging.

And most important, each and every one of us, young people and youth leaders alike, must feel acceptance and understanding. We need desperately to be able to share our thoughts and feelings with one person, or several, who really understand. We yearn for the deep relief of knowing that we can be ourselves, secure in the knowledge that says, "This person is with me. He accepts how I feel!"

COMMUNICATING LOVE TO YOUR YOUNG PEOPLE

To be effective as positive disciplinarians, we must love each of our young people just the way they are. In order to love them we must get to know them beyond surface relationships. We need to be their friends. I respond more favorably to someone who is correcting me if they have taken the time beforehand to get to know me. If I sense they have made an effort to move past the superficial relationship of passing in the church halls to getting to know the inner me, I will listen more intently to what they have to say regarding my behavior. I know that they genuinely care about me as an individual.

A good friend of mine, Dick Gibson, described in the November/December 1992 issue of *Group* magazine 55 ways to love your kids. These are great things to do when the time comes to put up or shut up in loving your kids:

1. Remember names. Few things leave a more lasting impression on kids than your ability to call them by name!

2. Meet at the kids' level. Position yourself to communicate at eye level. Also take care that your vocabulary is easily understood by your teenagers.

3. Send birthday cards. Who do young people get cards from? Immediate family, extended relatives and close friends. Why not add your name to that list?

4. Invite them along. "Never go anywhere alone." Asking someone to join you confirms their worth to you. And it's a great chance to share informally and to role model the Christian life.

5. Be in touch. How many kids suffered through another week without positive physical contact? Expressions as simple as a hand on the shoulder or a "holy hug" can prove your concern.

6. Respond to absences. Many young people drop out when they feel unneeded or unimportant. When you follow up with them, it communicates their value to you and the group.

7. Forgive and forget. "Love keeps no record of wrongs" (1 Cor. 13:5). If you model authentic forgiveness it'll give your kids the courage to do the same.

8. Recognize accomplishments. Look for opportunities to applaud your group members. Spread the word to family and friends that you want to know about this inside information.

9. Write encouraging notes. Kids love to get mail, so send them brief postcards or letters. Express your confidence in them and reaffirm your availability.

10. Offer support in a crisis. You're never more needed than when your teenagers face trouble. When kids face unexpected pregnancy, abuse, crime, death, or rejection, your active concern can impact them for a lifetime.

11. Recognize personality changes. Abrupt shifts from normal behavior patterns may be signals for help. Don't hesitate to share your concerns.

12. Follow up prayer requests. Ask for progress reports on prayer concerns. This reminds your kids that you take their spiritual life seriously and helps them recognize God's provision.

13. Use the telephone. How often do you phone your teenagers for no reason? Call just to say "Hi!"

14. Go to their "natural habitat." Your presence on your group members' turf is significant. So go to school events or schedule a visit at their work place.

15. Open your home. Occasionally ask kids to join you at home apart from regular group activities.

16. Confront in love. Authentic concern sometimes says, "I care for you too much to let that continue." Your willingness to deal with tough issues reveals the true nature of your commitment (Heb. 12:5-11).

17. Listen. You don't need all the answers, just two good ears. Empower your teenagers to talk through their problems with someone they can trust.

18. Answer questions. Young people have difficulty interpreting the mixed messages they receive. If they ask, it's because they trust you. Don't be afraid to respond honestly, even in sensitive areas.

19. Say "I love you!" These words can never be said too often. Say them personally, sincerely and individually.

20. Affirm spiritual growth. Everyone can use a spiritual "pat on the back." Commend godly character you observe.

21. "Unwrap" kids' giftedness. When you detect latent talents or abilities in your kids, give them the encouragement and opportunity to explore those gifts.

22. Expect the best. Young people will settle to your level of expectation so aim high.

23. Accept them as they are. Teenagers are in transition from childhood to adulthood, and they can act like either at any moment. Be patient; God's not finished with them (or you, for that matter).

24. Focus on their interests. Investigate your group members' hobbies and ask for pointers. They'll be happy to oblige, and you'll gain new insights into them.

25. Be available. Inform your group that you're accessible when they need you (remember to tell them when you're not available too). You have lost an opportunity if they weather their storms alone.

26. Laugh together. Don't be so serious that you miss humorous moments.

27. Cultivate kids' opinions. Invite honest feedback and keep an open mind. God may want your young people to teach you something.

28. Be real. Your teenagers hunger for relationships with people who have the confidence to be themselves.

29. Be a "soft touch." When you can, participate in your kids' fund-raisers. To avoid poverty, I purchase from *only* the first group member who asks me to.

30. Speak first. Initiating conversation can be difficult for shy or new group members. Make them feel important by speaking to them first.

31. Give positive reinforcement. Some young people are lightning rods for criticism. So look for something praiseworthy in every group member.

32. Keep confidences. Develop a reputation as someone who's reliable with confidential information. Nothing is more destructive to your credibility than breaking a trust.

33. Share "good news." When group members make the news, mail them the clippings. Even if their parents already have a supply for the relatives, they'll appreciate your thoughtfulness.

34. Seek sanctuary. Your meetings should not be a battleground for personal disputes. Place a high priority on emotional security and acceptance for everyone.

35. Be dependable. How's your track record for consistency? If you're reliable in the small things you'll be rewarded with greater confidence (Matt. 25:14-28).

36. Be a servant. Greatness, as Jesus demonstrated, is expressed through service. Your group will reflect this truth to the extent they observe it in you (Matt. 10:24-25).

37. Send postcards. When you travel, mail postcards about your experiences to your group members. Let them know that even though you're away, they're still on your mind.

38. Smile. Your smile expresses openness and approachability.

39. Watch your tone of voice. Clear communication is made up of the words we choose and how we express them. Take care that your tone reflects concern and support.

40. Be attentive. It's frustrating to talk with someone whose actions demonstrate they're not interested. Make sure your body language reflects concern.

41. Support through prayer. Select two or three group members to pray for every week. Inform them in advance and ask for special needs or requests.

42. Maintain eye contact. The eyes are a window to the soul. So let your kids see your compassion in your eyes.

43. Watch your words. Real affection is often exercised through what we determine *not* to say. Your careless remarks could leave lasting scars.

44. Post kids' pictures. Ask each group member for a school photo. Exhibit these photos in a high-profile place.

45. Give kids respect. This is a "boomerang principle"—give and you will receive in return.

46. Take them seriously. Any problem, no matter how trivial it may seem to you, is your kids' biggest concern at the moment. Don't brush it off.

47. Admit your mistakes. Don't be fooled. We're usually the last to acknowledge what others already know.

48. Avoid church/school conflicts. Arbitrary scheduling that forces kids to choose between church and school activities is unfair.

49. Foster teamwork. Although your role will always involve overseeing the tasks at hand, don't lose touch with the crew. Serving together in the trenches builds camaraderie.

50. Invest your time in them. There's no substitute for just being together. This life-to-life interaction is the essence of discipleship.

51. Smooth "rough" edges. Do you have kids who lack social graces or need help with personal hygiene? It's awkward, but that's what friends are for.

52. Visit them at home. A young person's room is his or her corner of the world and your turnstile to it. Make an appointment and ask for a "guided tour."

53. Empathize. Empathy is "feeling your pain in my heart." Isn't this how Jesus expressed his love for us? (Phil. 2:6-7) Remember what it was like to be a kid.

54. Play together. If your teenagers would rather watch than participate, help them rediscover the joy of play. Choose activities that stress total group participation.

55. Resist favoritism. If pressed, you'd admit feeling "closer" to some kids than others. Budget your time and attention to everyone equally.

NOW ASK YOURSELF

1. What is your motivation behind having well-disciplined young people?

2. Besides "boring," describe what your youth group would be like if you only had mature and cooperative young people?

3. What are your expectations of your young people?

4. Who in your life encouraged you to pursue your dreams as a teen? How did they do it?

5. What are some overused negative phrases that you need to cut back on or eliminate?

6. Call a young person and let him or her know you appreciate him or her. (Be specific as to why.)

7. Each of us wears different hats in youth ministry. Overall, how do the young people in your youth group see you? Are you content with this opinion? If not, how can you change it?

A. Police officer	E. Just one of the kids
B. Fire fighter	F. Mother or father
C. Clown	G. Baby-sitter
D. Scholar	

8. What positive, desirable qualities do you have in your life? What areas do you need to work on?

A. Modeling	G. Allowing them to fail
B. Honesty	H. Overlooking without ignoring
C. Wisdom	I. Sense of humor
D. Patience	J. Admitting failures
E. Cooperation	K. Loving
F. Consistency	

9. Is there a weak link on your team? How can this tactfully be corrected?

10. Are you able to laugh at yourself? Are you fun to be with? If not, what can you do to change?

11. Is your youth group a loving group? Do your kids feel wanted?

"Norman, it's been my conviction for some time that you've lost control of the high-schoolers."

RULES AND GUIDELINES

Without rules you have anarchy. But with too many rules you can deaden a young person's spirit or incite rebellion. Rules without relationships lead to rebellion. Openness may be the key to finding a balance between these extremes.

The best kind of discipline is that in which the young person has a voice. We may get good behavior faster if we operate from a position of unquestionable authority, but it won't be as healthy or long-lasting. Young people should be encouraged to participate in the rule-making process. Recognize that each event can be seen from different points of view. It is so easy to fall into the myopic trap of believing that yours is the only valid perspective, but your students have a lot to contribute too. Teenagers are attempting to gain independence and autonomy, and enlisting their help in designing rules will help them mature and develop self-discipline.

BRAINSTORMING

It's good to let the adult leaders and the teens work together to establish the guidelines or rules. Both should share their expectations and try to arrive at a compromise. Although this can be a difficult and frustrating process, it's worth it—for it lets the young people know that the leaders have confidence in them. Once the guidelines are established, they need to be posted so everyone is aware of them.

Have the youth group engage in a time of brainstorming together to determine some of the rules. The term "brainstorming" and the technique of using it were invented by Dr. Alex Osborn, who first applied it to generating ideas to solve problems in business. Unfortunately, he pointed out, many times when three or four people sit down to solve a problem, someone will come up with an idea and someone else will say, "No, that won't work, because. . . ." This sequence of idea and rebuttal will take place a number of times. The net effect is to inhibit people from coming up with new ideas.

So the first rule of brainstorming is that nobody is allowed to criticize anybody else's ideas. There are no limits on the ideas that may be generated. Even though an idea may be impractical, it may stimulate someone else in the group to come up with a different idea that will work.

Explain to your youth group how brainstorming works. Then have each member suggest as many ideas as possible, while a note taker writes them all down and numbers them. There is no special time limit on this, but you probably shouldn't go over twenty minutes or under five minutes.

Once all the ideas are written down, go over them one by one to try to find one or more solutions to a particular problem. The solution must be one that everyone can agree to. Obviously all the rules for a youth group should not be determined by the young people themselves; furthermore, on the rules that are decided by the group, I don't recommend voting, because with voting someone wins and someone loses. The group is to think through what will be best for its welfare. Using this method, each young person is motivated to carry out the rule since he has participated in the rule-making process. The rule has not been thrust upon him by the youth group leaders.

The use of this brainstorming technique usually results in a reduction of hostility on the part of the young person. Since he must agree on the rule, he is less likely to walk away angry, secretly resolving to sabotage the group's rules.

Most young people develop rules much more demanding than those imposed by adults. And when the young people make the rules they are much more easily enforced, interpreted, and supported.

In fact, teens will often set a harsher discipline for themselves than you would, if given the chance. Most young people don't want to have undesirable qualities. If you have a reasonably good relationship with them, it is uncanny how they will come up with something stricter than what you had in mind. And they will probably learn more from their self-imposed discipline too. Ask them what would be a fair and motivating punishment (and reward) in specific situations.

Here is a composite list of rules that young people and adult leaders have drawn up:

High School Rules and Guidelines and Miscellaneous Bits of Information

1. When we go on activities, all students ride the church bus or church vans. No student is allowed to drive.

2. All students are to go to their Bible school class for their grade on Sunday mornings and not change classes.

3. All students attending church activities are expected to participate in that activity and not "hang around" outside the church building.

4. When returning from an activity, the time to meet at the church bus or van will be repeated several times. If a student is late and it is a safe environment, the student will be left and the parents called to come and pick up their high schooler.

5. When we return from an activity, parents are to pick up their high schoolers at the time stated.

6. Any youth activities that are planned by students, parents, or teachers that appear to be sponsored by Eastside Christian Church must be cleared with the youth minister.

7. Graduation takes place in June at our church. During the summer the graduating seniors are to attend the college activities only.

8. When groups go to Tijuana to distribute food and clothing, no one is allowed

to purchase fireworks or any illegal materials.

9. In the worship service, we expect our students to have an attitude of respect and reverence. No food or drinks are to be brought into the auditorium during worship service. All hats are to be taken off during the worship service.

10. If a student wants to teach in Bible school, it must be cleared with the youth minister.

11. If any student wants to counsel at a camp, they must also attend the camp designed for their age group as a camper.

12. Abstain from wrestling in any of the church buildings. God wants you to use your energy more constructively (at least outside). WWF is available for any would-be grapplers.

13. Abstain from throwing objects. God doesn't want you to tear a rotator cuff by heaving a projectile across the room. It is not God's will to knock someone's face off at youth group.

14. Listen to all adult youth workers at all times. Praise God for sending these "angels" to look out for your best interests. When they speak, listen.

15. Abstain from any kissing, affectionate hugging, hand holding, etc. during youth activities. We want you to concentrate on the Lord and his youth group while you are at church-sponsored events. No making out allowed in church vans also.

16. Take care of all church property (games, walls, books, vans, etc.). If you break the church property (thus, the Lord's property) while messing around, expect to fix it or buy a new one.

17. Refrain from running in all church buildings.

18. Have fun in the church facilities. But remember this rule: Treat others as Christ would, and treat others' belongings as Christ wants you to. Rules are made for our benefit, not to hinder our fun!

19. In conversations, if you disagree, attack the idea, not the person.

20. No whining.

21. Adult sponsors have the final say in the kind of music played and listened to at youth activities.

22. No alcohol, cigarettes, drugs, pornography, chew, or cigars at youth activities.

23. No obscene language.

A fair rule for an individual is a guideline, boundary, or limit which takes into account his or her background, experience, age, and personality, and which helps him or her mature, moving toward becoming a whole person.

A fair rule for a group is similar, with the very important exception that more than one person is involved. A group rule must take into consideration the various individuals involved (their uniqueness, needs, backgrounds, histories, etc.) and the special personality of the group as a whole. It is also important to consider the purpose of the group and the fact that rules must be consistently and uniformly enforced.

Here are some questions which will help you determine which of your rules are fair and which of them are not.

1. Is it important (or just a personal preference)? In other words, does your rule reflect your ministry priorities or does it merely reflect your personal biases?

2. Will it help or hinder your relationships?

3. Will it help the young person mature as a whole person? Consider how the rule effects the mental, social, physical, and spiritual areas of the individual's life.

4. Is it reasonable? Understanding where the person is developmentally and socially, can you expect him or her to accept this rule? Is it consistent and within his or her ability to obey?

5. Is it specific and clearly stated? In other words, does the young person understand what you really mean and what the limits are?

While young people should have a voice in making the rules that apply to them, they are expected to follow the rules which are established. The young people do not decide whether or not rules, once established, should be enforced. They may choose to disobey the rules; this choice is open to all. But they have to accept the consequences of their choice.

STATE RULES POSITIVELY

A positively stated rule implies to young people that you expect them to function in a mature and responsible way. Avoid overusing the word "don't" when stating rules; a rule that specifically addresses a negative behavior tends to communicate a negative expectation. "Don't talk while someone else is talking," tends to imply, "I expect you to be rude and interrupt people; don't do it."

Make your communication as positive as realistically possible. It is easy to get into the habit of starting sentences with "I wish you wouldn't . . ." "Do you really have to . . ." "Isn't there any other way . . ." "Must you . . ." and other endless phrases that immediately set up the young person to feel defensive.

Positively stated rules serve as an overall expectation. Positively stated rules inform young people that they are with a youth leader who will demand their best—who will not tolerate anything less, and who believes they will give their best.

Make sure everyone understands how your youth group will be conducted, along with your expectations. This should be done as soon as possible after the new freshmen are brought into your group either at the beginning or end of summer. This is important because it allows you to clarify expectations prior to any opportunities for misbehavior.

KEEP RULES TO A MINIMUM

Don't set more rules than you are prepared to enforce—that will only cause you heartache. Rules should *not* be made to be broken. They should be made to be kept. Furthermore, they should set limits on behavior, not opinion.

Because the potential list of misbehavior is endless, negatively stated rules also tend to be unmanageable. Massive "don't" lists make it difficult to respond consistently to misbehavior. I always thought it was ironic that, at summer camp, the director would stand up the first day to welcome the new group of campers, and the first thing out of his mouth would be all the things they couldn't do. After about fifteen minutes of this huge list of don'ts, he usually closed with, "But have a great time at camp." These same negative expectations can be stated in a positive way which takes very little extra effort. Simply describe appropriate behavior rather than inappropriate behavior. Young people need to know what they can do as well as what they can't.

Rules are like winter clothing. If you put them on all at once, especially before it is necessary, you can smother. Just as it's easy to make a young person frustrated from too many layers of unnecessary clothing, it's easy to lay on too many unnecessary rules.

The greater the number of rules and orders you have, the more your young people will disobey. This is not a mere matter of arithmetic. A fundamental drive in each of us wants to do things for ourselves in our own way. Young people have an inborn, life-giving aggressiveness that makes them fight to overcome obstacles. They seem to know that sooner or later they must stand on their own feet and that they need the experience of trying things out themselves while you are there to help them if they fall. But if you are the obstacle, if you block their plans and direct their every move, if you make rules to cover all contingencies, they either forget the rules or rebel against them.

To be effective, rules must be as follows:
- **Simple.** Young people must be able to repeat rules and understand them.
- **Firm.** Rules are not bent by a flimsy excuse.
- **Fair.** Rules are applied equally to all young people.
- **Flexible.** Rules can be adjusted occasionally to fit the circumstances.

BE SPECIFIC

If a rule is well-defined, a young person knows immediately when it is broken. Youth leaders often assume that their young people know what is expected without setting the standards. Many a youth worker has been heard to say, "Well, he ought to know that's what I meant." Young people are no better at mind reading than their youth leaders are.

If you want things to be done a specific way, then give specific instructions. If it doesn't matter how things are done, as long as they are done, then you need not be specific.

In making rules, define what is important and stress it. Decide also what is unimportant and ignore it. Too many youth workers exhaust themselves and wear out their relationships with young people because they expend far too much time and energy focusing on minor issues.

In describing how you want young people to behave, provide as much detailed information as possible. Young people have had many youth leaders and authority figures over the years. Some allow talking, others do not. Some youth leaders want students to raise their hands, others do not. Some let them bring radios on activities, others do not. Each individual youth leader must clarify his or her expectations.

Provide explicit information on how you want students to interact with each other and with you. Introduce each activity by telling your young people whether they may talk to each other and, if so, how loudly, about what topics, and for how long. Some students will talk during the entire Bible study if they are simply told that talking is allowed. It is important to clarify exactly what you mean.

Suppose you say, "I would appreciate it if you would be back to the van at 9 o'clock tonight." Are your young people likely to believe that they *must* be back to the van at 9 o'clock, or that you would merely show appreciation if they came back at 9 o'clock?

Be clear and specific in your communication. Major youth group blowups often are the result of unclear communication or statements that are too general.

Begin your directions by telling young people what to do using a firm and resolute voice that sounds as though you mean what you say. Use words describing an element of time (now, never, always) or a verb (stop, quit, don't, be, take, make, do). Add when and how often you want the rule obeyed. The fewer words you use the better. Extra words cause blank stares, angry confrontations, misunderstood directions, and a host of other problems.

A major difference between effective and less effective youth workers is the degree to which they have defined and communicated their expectations of young people. An effective youth worker knows exactly how he wants students to behave and what he hopes to accomplish during every activity.

Identify every type of activity that might be included in your ministry. Design rules and expectations on the basis of this list.

Young people and youth leader interactions can be improved only when you have established clear expectations for teen behavior. Young people cannot be self-disciplined if they do not know what is acceptable and what is not acceptable. Clear expectations will allow you to respond consistently to behavior, and will give young people a chance to demonstrate their willingness to cooperate.

Dr. James Dobson gives an example of a teenager whose mother's *no* meant *maybe*, and how these unclear expectations can cause difficulties.

> Betty Sue is an argumentative teenager. She never takes "no" for an answer. She is very cantankerous; in fact, her father says the only time she is ever homesick is when she is at home. Whenever her mother is not sure about whether she wants to let Betty go to a party or a ball game, she will first tell her she *can't* go. By saying an initial "no," Betty's mom doesn't commit herself to a "yes" before she's had a chance to think it over. She can always change her mind from negative to positive, but it is difficult to go the other way. However, what does this system tell Betty? She can see that "no" really means "maybe." The harder she argues and complains, the more likely she is to obtain the desired "yes."[16]

Many youth workers make the same mistake as Betty Sue's mother. They allow themselves to be swayed when group members whine, argue, or beg. Be sure to think through the stand you want to take on an issue, then stick with it.

Being specific is also important because young people have a remarkable capacity for finding loopholes in or getting around the rules that youth workers impose on them. "No talking" is answered with "We're not talking—we're whispering." If the youth leader makes the fatal mistake of pointing out that "whispering is just quiet talking," the young people involved will raise the level of discussion to "Why can't we whisper? We're not bothering anybody." All of this leads to a dialogue that ends up with the young person winning because now everybody is "talking." Lee Strobel sometimes uses this example:

> I pretend that my daughter, Alison, and her boyfriend are going out for a Coke on a school night, and I say to her: "You must be home before eleven." How would you interpret that? It's pretty straightforward, isn't it?
>
> This would never happen, but suppose it gets to be 10:45 and the two of them are still having a great time at Portillo's Hot Dog Stand. They aren't really anxious to end the evening, so suddenly they begin to have difficulty interpreting my instructions.
>
> They say, "What did he really mean when he said, '*You* must be home before eleven'? Did he literally mean *us*, or was he talking about *you* in a general sense, like people in general? Was he saying, in effect, 'As a general rule, people must be home before eleven'? Or was he just making the observation that, 'Generally, people are in their homes before eleven'? I mean, he wasn't very clear, was he?
>
> "And what did he mean by, 'You *must* be home before eleven'? Would a loving father be so adamant and inflexible? He probably means it as a suggestion. I know he loves me, so isn't it implicit that he wants me to have a good time? And if I am having fun, then he wouldn't want me to end the evening so soon.
>
> "And what did he mean by, 'You must be *home* before eleven'? He didn't specify whose home. It could be anybody's home. Maybe he meant it figuratively. Remember the old saying, 'Home is where the heart is'? My heart is here at Portillo's, so doesn't that mean I'm already home?
>
> "And what did he really mean when he said, 'You must be home before *eleven*'? Did he mean that in an exact, literal sense? Besides, he never specified 11P.M. or 11A.M. and he wasn't really clear on whether he was talking about Central Standard Time or Pacific Time. I mean, it's still only quarter to seven in Honolulu. And as a matter of fact, when you think about it, it's always before eleven. Whatever time it is, it's always before the next eleven. So with all of these ambiguities, we can't really be sure what he meant at all. If he can't make himself clear, we certainly can't be held responsible."

RULES MUST BE REASONABLE

No one is perfect; don't expect it of yourself or of your young people. Don't force your own unrealized expectations upon your young people.

We have to begin by making sure our expectations for their behavior are realistic and age appropriate. If we expect a group of junior highers to sit in a classroom with their hands in their laps and their lips tightly zipped, then we're not being realistic. In *The Exuberant Years* (John Knox, 1971), author Ginny Ward Holderness admits that "junior highers are noisy, restless, and mischievous. There are bound to be problems." David Shaheen agrees. "Their preoccupation with self can cause several mood changes within a short period of time," he writes in *Growing a Junior High Ministry* (Group Books,

1986). "There is no predictable pattern to the way they feel. The same person can be loud and rowdy, or quiet and shy, in a matter of minutes."

In addition to kids' generally high-energy level and moodiness, there's the problem of different levels of maturity among kids of the same chronological age. There can be as much as a six-year difference in the maturity level of kids in the same grade.

With these considerations in mind, we need to develop practical, realistic expectations for behavior. We somehow have to differentiate between behavior that simply irritates us and behavior that hurts either the individual or the group.

A rule should be reasonable. It should actually make the environment more comfortable for the young people and the youth leaders. The rule should be one that the young person is capable of following. It's not practical to make a rule that the young person is not physically or mentally able to obey.

When we are unable to gain a sense of achievement in life, as when we feel incapable of carrying out tasks that lie before us, we also are bothered. Anyone who has tried a job that's too difficult knows this only too well. Whenever a person is expected to do things which she is actually not able to do, she feels lost. She feels overpowered and small and helpless—perhaps even panicky and embittered. "I'm incapable, so what's the use?" Don't burden your young people with unreasonable rules which make them feel this way.

WHEN RULES NEED TO BE CHANGED

The value of the rule is to serve the group, not the reverse. Often the group will recognize the wisdom of changing its rules or their enforcement for the benefit of the total group. Rules should be reasonable and should be changed when conditions change. Whether the rules are written is less important than that they be specific, mutually agreed on, and tailored to the individual youth group.

At one time we had a rule that some of our high schoolers could drive their cars to and from activities away from the church if they proved to be responsible drivers. Eventually we decided as a group that this rule needed to be changed for two reasons: (1) It was difficult to determine which high schoolers were responsible drivers, and the question prompted a number of heated conversations. (2) Our group began to stay in cliques because kids wanted to drive or ride with their friends. Those who did not know someone who drove and had to ride in one of the church vans felt like losers. We felt it was important for all of us to go in a church bus for the sake of unity and safety. The kids agreed, even though some of the older ones enjoyed being able to drive, so the rule was changed.

It is reasonable to relax rules as young people become more responsible. All rules should be examined carefully. Rules considered necessary should be enforced, and the others should be dropped.

NOW ASK YOURSELF

1. Place a mark on the line showing how much involvement your students have in rule-making.

A little_____A lot

2. Enlist your young people's help in designing rules. What are their opinions about the rules you now have? What changes do they want to make?

3. State positively, in writing, the rules you have for your youth group and list the reasons for them. Are there any that are unnecessary? Are there some that need to be changed?

*"I like being a youth pastor. I really do. It's just that...
well, every once in a while I'd like to run over the
junior high group with a steamroller."*

CONSEQUENCES

Rules will have no weight with young people unless specific consequences for rule-breaking are established along with the rules. One type of consequence that has worked effectively for our group involves denying the young person a future fun activity with the youth group.

It's not always easy to enforce consequences, but it must be done. One example of this from my experience occurred on youth choir tour when two choir members were overheard telling derogatory racial jokes while changing clothes in the men's restroom before the concert. The visitor who heard the boys reported the incident to me and then left because of the boys' insulting language.

I confronted the two boys, hoping they would be sorry for what had happened. They were not. In fact, they could see no problem in putting people down in a joking manner— no matter whom it offended. They felt that if the visitor couldn't handle these jokes, that was *his* problem. Needless to say, I was greatly disappointed by their response. I told them that the next day, when the rest of the youth choir went to an amusement park, the two boys would be helping adult sponsors wash choir outfits at a local laundromat.

The boys knew from the instructions before the tour what was expected of them and the consequences for violating the rules. I think if they had been sincerely sorry for the negative influence they had on this visitor, I would have handled the consequences in a different manner with a less severe form of discipline. These two choir members were not thrilled with me (in fact, they were angry), but they knew I had played fair with them. Enforcing rules won't win you popularity contests, but without real consequences, rules are worthless.

Remember, you don't want to reel off a long list of don'ts before each activity, but it is important to review rules and consequences. If young people have no idea how you will respond to misbehavior, they will test you to find out what will happen. If this occurs, you are forced to either invent a consequence on the spot, or else overlook the misbehavior. If you implement a consequence for the misbehavior, your young people may feel, justifiably, that they have not been treated fairly. If you fail to implement a consequence, your young people will feel that misbehavior is acceptable. It is obviously better to discuss the consequences for certain behavior beforehand. Young people need to be informed.

The list of misbehaviors should not be posted. Post your positive expectations if you have to post something. Posting negative behaviors can serve as a reminder to some young people to engage in misbehavior. Simply inform the youth group about consequences for misbehavior.

HOW TO CARRY OUT CONSEQUENCES

Discipline techniques must show your young people that you will not tolerate certain behavior. At the same time, discipline that severely embarrasses students may cut down on misbehavior, but can also destroy any possibility of a positive relationship between youth worker and young person. A young person who has been humiliated by a youth leader is unlikely ever to do well for that youth worker again and will not do more than the bare minimum required to avoid further humiliation.

It is important to remain as unemotional as possible when following through on discipline. Your staying calm basically demonstrates to a young person that power is not gained through misbehavior.

When I am tired or emotionally exhausted I tend to overreact with discipline. All of us at times have "lost our cool" or "gone off the deep end," and I'm no exception. One particular time my overreaction really backfired. There was a certain young man who would come into our high school Sunday School class halfway through the meeting, look around the room for about three minutes, and then leave. This went on for three Sundays, and it bothered me that this person refused to join us. I meant to talk to him about it but had not had the chance.

On the fourth Sunday, I was rushed and not well prepared, and halfway through the lesson when this same young person walked into the room, I let him have it with both barrels, giving him a piece of my mind I couldn't afford to lose. I even surprised myself with how angry I got. The boy kept trying to say something, but I wouldn't let him get a word in edgewise. Finally he blurted out, "I'm not in this class! My job is to come in each week and take attendance."

Boy, did I look dumb. The rest of the kids looked at me and then at him. Fortunately this boy was more together than I was. He accepted my apology, and when I started to laugh at how silly I must have looked, he joined in. Soon the entire class was laughing. I had just learned a lesson about staying calm and not jumping to conclusions.

WARN ONCE AND ONLY ONCE

Establish definite policies for rule violation and make sure the young people know them. Have one warning and only one warning; if that doesn't stop the misbehavior, then be sure to follow through, otherwise it will be a battle of wills. The next step in the process involves bringing the offender to a higher authority—the youth minister or church board official. If the behavior continues, then call the parents. Always approach the young person first (before you contact parents) and explain what will happen if he or she doesn't straighten out. If a serious situation comes up where the parents must be notified, I always give the young person the chance to explain it to the parents first. I will give them a few days to talk to their parents, and if they don't break the news to Mom and Dad after a specified time, I expect the student to join me for my talk with the parents.

The key is to deal with problems quickly and quietly. Use the lowest level of control necessary to eliminate the problem. If you have a tendency to overreact, don't give in to it.

NATURAL AND LOGICAL CONSEQUENCES

Adult life is structured along the lines of natural and logical consequences. Too many traffic tickets lead to a high insurance premium (logical consequences). Poor personal hygiene leads to poor personal health (natural consequences). In natural consequences there is a built-in consequence that naturally happens. In logical consequences the consequence is built-in by an authority figure.

Dr. Rudolph Dreikurs is usually associated with popularizing the concept of logical consequences. In Scripture, logical consequences are described by God throughout Exodus 21–23. There God outlines a number of rules and consequences for breaking them. If a rule was broken accidentally (Ex. 22:5), then repayment was made on an equal basis. If a deliberate theft took place, repayment might range from four to five times the value of what was stolen (Ex. 22:1).

The term "logical consequence" gets its name from a logical relationship between what is expected and what takes place. Think of it as an "if/then" relationship. "If you don't, then you won't." Logical consequences can also have a positive result. "If you continue to work hard, then you will be given more responsibility," or "If you continue to save your money, you will have enough to buy that car you wanted by the time you reach eighteen."

Many things in our lives operate by the standards of logical consequences. If we want our young people to become competent in dealing with the workaday world, then it is vital for them to learn how to deal with the consequences. The concepts of schedules and promptness depend on logical consequences. How many of you have remembered late Saturday afternoon that your Sunday outfit was at the cleaners? Then you rushed to the cleaners only to arrive five minutes after they closed for the weekend. That's how it works in real life.

The basic principle of natural consequences is to let your young people learn from experience, wherever possible, when it cannot possibly result in serious injury. It's simply letting nature run its course. If the natural consequences of an action are pleasant, the young person will continue to act that way. If the natural consequences are unpleasant, the young person will be motivated to change his or her actions.

The temptation is often great to protect your young people from unpleasant natural consequences. But if you protect them they will not be motivated to change. They need to learn to take care of themselves. So giving them the chance to learn natural consequences ultimately boosts their self-confidence and self-esteem.

Becky was responsible for publicity in our youth group. We had an important activity coming up that we hoped would attract a lot of non-Christian kids. But Becky only completed half of the publicity and left it unfinished with a note on my desk. She was hoping

I would finish it.

I called her home and left a message with her mother, explaining that the publicity was Becky's responsibility, and that if she didn't do it, it wouldn't get done. Becky didn't complete it, and only half the number of kids we were expecting showed up.

The following Monday, Becky came into my office. I asked her what happened. She explained that she felt she had let down the whole group. I agreed with her and asked what she thought she should do next.

"Maybe I should just quit," she responded.

"Quit? Quit!" I replied.

"Well, maybe I shouldn't quit," said Becky.

We talked about responsibility and commitment. Becky saw how she could change her priorities and schedule in order to get things done. We prayed together that God would use her. Becky was a dynamite publicity chairperson from that day on. I could always count on her.

Becky is now married and is an active leader of a large "young married" group at our church. She and her husband are also getting ready to go to the mission field. Becky learned by being allowed to fail and experience the consequences of the failure.

Letting young people learn the consequences of some of their behaviors helps them learn to be more responsible. Young people who are protected and don't learn that there are consequences to bad choices learn the hard way, when they are adults, that poor choices result in pain and suffering. Only in adulthood the pain is greater and there is more at stake.

DISCUSSION AFTER A PROBLEM HAS OCCURRED

Discussing problems with young people after they have occurred can sometimes help to reduce future problem behavior. Discussions can help young people recognize that they have control over their actions, and that in any given situation, there are different ways they could choose to respond.

Plan to discuss the problem when you and the young person involved are calm. This generally requires a cooling-off period. You may choose to discuss inappropriate behavior the day after it happens. If you discuss the problem immediately after the misbehavior, some young people may be reinforced for misbehaving because they've gotten your attention or gotten you to stop teaching and have a discussion. Delaying the discussion for a limited time reduces the likelihood of this problem.

Confront the young person when you have planned out what you want to say. Select a time and neutral location where no other teens are present. You might take him or her to a fast food restaurant at a time when the restaurant isn't busy. Let the young person know that you still care for and love him even though you don't care for the act he or she has committed. It is necessary to separate the *deed* from the *doer*.

Inform the young person that you will contact her parents if she continues to engage in misbehavior. End the discussion by communicating a positive expectation of future behavior.

If the problem is with one to three young people, arrange to have your discussion with only those involved in the problem. However, if the problem occurs with several young people, hold your discussion with the entire youth group. Even though the majority of the youth group is not involved, the problem becomes a youth group problem if several young people are involved.

Begin the discussion by explaining to the young people how you perceive the problem. Give the young people an opportunity to explain the problem as they see it. Do not allow the discussion to degenerate into a session of accusations and denials. Establish the basic events that led to the problem and what happened.

Help young people to explore other ways of dealing with a similar situation. Young people frequently know only one way to respond to a situation.

WHAT IS YOUR PROBLEM-SOLVING STYLE?

Which of these best describes your style of handling problems in your youth group?

- **Deny the problem exists.** "There is nothing wrong with my youth group," or "I don't have any problems."
- **Appeal to authority.** "In our church we know how to handle young people like that," or "My professor always said to handle young people this way," or "The church board ought to deal with this."
- **Minimize the problem.** "There's really nothing to worry about. I'll have this straightened out in no time," or "It's a phase they are going through."
- **Personal satisfaction.** "In my youth group these young people had better do what I tell them to do. I don't have the time or energy to put up with any foolishness."
- **Pure empiricist.** "Before I can do anything, I'll need to know the facts and only the facts."
- **Intuitive.** "I just know inside of me that something is wrong."[17]

PARENTS CAN BE PARTNERS IN DISCIPLINE

If parents are supportive and interested, parental contacts can be a useful strategy for eliminating behavior problems. Even if the parents are not supportive, or have little impact on the young person's behavior, the parental contact is important.

Parents have a right to know if there are problems with their kids in the church, and you have the right to assistance from parents. By working together you can solve many disruptive behaviors before they escalate into major problems.

We had one girl at a youth meeting who decided to sneak off with another friend and do some drinking. When they came back, our adult sponsors could smell the liquor on her breath. The sponsors talked to her but did not tell her parents. With hindsight I now see that, on this particular occasion, it might have been wiser to meet with the young lady and her parents, though it would have been painful for all those involved. In this case the parents are terrific parents and would have handled the situation maturely. Instead, we decided to play parent and handle it ourselves. Later the girl's parents did find out about the incident and were greatly disappointed that we had not informed them of the situation.

When speaking to parents, clearly and firmly state the problem the young person is having. Tell the parents that you need their support. When you contact a parent regarding a problem with a son or daughter, and that parent supports your efforts, take the time to show your appreciation. Thank parents for their support by sending them a note or making a quick call.

Parents are a potential ally during flareups. Such mutual helping would be in sharp contrast to the mutual blaming that often occurs when the young person is experiencing difficulty at church.

Parents need to know your expectations if they are to support you. You may want to send home a letter each year to the parents of all incoming group members, outlining your discipline plan.

Parents are accustomed to receiving only negative news when a youth worker contacts them. Send home some positive notes to parents if you have noticed improved behavior. It communicates to them that you have a positive attitude toward their son or daughter. It will also increase your chances of gaining parental support if there is a problem.

When problems do arise, document them. Keep detailed records of inappropriate behavior. Doing so will enable you to relate problems in a fair, nonjudgmental manner to parents.

One principal of a junior high school discovered by accident how to successfully discipline problem junior highers. "A kid came into my office whom I had talk(ed) to a number of times for minor discipline problems—talking in class, being late, not bringing materials, driving the teachers crazy," relates John Lazores of Wilson Junior High in Hamilton, Ohio. At one point Principal Lazores just got fed up and finally said, "The next time I see you, we're going to have your mother come in and see what we have to put up with all day." The reaction he got from the young person was, "Do anything you want, but don't have my mother come in."

But in his mother did come—and spent a full day in class. And since then about 60 parents have put in their time at Wilson. Results? Detentions are down from 20 per day to none on some days; expulsions have dropped from 120 per year to 11 since the program began last year. Said Lazores, "Kids who have seen other kids' parents in school stop causing problems because they don't want their own parents to sit with them all day."

But punishment is only one aspect of the program. "In education, we're only as effective as the parents," says Lazores, "and now we have parents who can call us once a week to check up on the kids' progress." The net result has been improved grades and behavior by kids, and greater involvement by parents.[18]

CONTRACTING

Most youth workers are unfamiliar with the term *contracting* as applied to youth worker/youth relationships. Of course, if we have bought a house, or an automobile, or even a stereo, we are familiar with contracts in the world of business. In business contracting, two people make an agreement. Party "A" promises to do something, and party "B" promises to do something in return.

As a discipline method in the youth group, contracting is based on exactly the same concept. The contract is a positive way of disciplining young people. Contracting involves negotiating between the youth worker and the youth, which results in a commitment on both sides.

A formal written contract is laid out between the young person and the youth worker. Although a contract can be purely verbal, there are several good reasons why a contract should be written down. An agreement that is written prevents misunderstanding and arguments about it later. It emphasizes the responsibility that the youth worker and the young person have to uphold their respective parts of the contract. The contract should include the following:

1. A brief overall statement of the teen's goal
2. What the young person should do, rather than what they should not do
3. Specific language that avoids vague, unclear items
4. How behavior will be evaluated and monitored
5. How long the contract will be in effect
6. The youth worker's responsibility

The following page shows an example of a contract used with a student who would not follow directions in a Sunday School class.

Contract Agreement

Student: Laurie Hanover
Youth Sponsor: Jane Cromwell
Specific Time: Sunday School hour

Behavior Expectations	Acceptable	Unacceptable
Listening to and following directions in class		
Talking to someone else when directions are being given in class		
Playing with any objects while youth sponsor talks		
Turning around in chair while directions are being given		
Keeping your hands and feet to yourself		
Wrestling, pushing, or nudging others		

Evaluation: Each week after Sunday School the sponsor and the student will get together to evaluate that Sunday's behavior. If, at the end of five weeks, there are no problems, the student will be allowed to participate in the Christmas All-Nighter (or whatever activity fits your group).

_____   _____
Student's Signature   *Sponsor's Signature*

CORPORAL PUNISHMENT

Corporal punishment is any kind of punishment that uses physical force against someone else. It can appear in the form of spanking with a belt or paddle. Or it could include hitting, ear-pulling, strong-arming, and so forth.

Mild corporal punishment to a teen is more of a joke than a punishment. Some group members are amused when they can "push a youth worker over the edge." Some students even consider it a status symbol—showing how "tough" they are by prompting physical punishment.

One inexperienced Sunday School teacher in another church depended on this method for controlling an unruly group of ninth-grade boys: when somebody got out of a hand, the teacher would bop the student on the head with a foam rubber bat. Of course, it didn't really hurt. But because the students were being treated as children, this approach didn't work. Instead of preventing problems, this method caused kids to act like they wanted punishment—and laugh when they got it!

Corporal punishment has severe drawbacks as a consequence for misbehavior. Corporal punishment on teens can be very demeaning. It goes beyond embarrassment to the point of being humiliating. There are too many other methods of dealing with discipline to use this. I don't even recommend it as a last resort.

The final compelling drawback against using corporal punishment with teens is that it provides young people with a model of aggression. It is teaching young people that you use physical violence whenever you want someone to behave differently. This implies that the person with the most power is the person who is right. Youth groups must provide a model that teaches young people to work out disagreements intelligently rather than physically.

YOU MAY LOSE A FEW

Before we leave consequences for misbehavior, there is one other consequence of using discipline in youth groups in the church. You may lose some young people. I think I would rather run the risk of losing a few young people than face the certainty of damaging them all by not using any discipline. How can we teach respect for God by allowing chaos to reign in His house? Learning is impossible in an atmosphere of disorder. A permissive attitude toward group anarchy is the most certain way to guarantee the failure of your objectives.

NOW ASK YOURSELF

1. Do your young people know the consequences for breaking the rules? If not, how can you let them know in a positive manner?

2. What are some natural consequences you have observed in your youth group over the previous month?

3. What is the difference between natural and logical consequences?

4. What is your problem-solving style, and why?

A. Deny the problem exists

B. Appeal to authority

C. Minimize the problem

D. Personal satisfaction

E. Pure empiricist

F. Intuitive

5. How can you inform/involve parents in the area of discipline with your young people?

6. Do you think spanking is a way to curtail misbehavior at any age? If so, at what age should it cease, and why? By parents? By youth leaders?

While counseling at junior-high camp, Steve hears that still, small voice calling him to a senior pastorate.

PRAISE: CATCH THEM DOING SOMETHING RIGHT

Working with loud, restless, adventurous youth is difficult, but I prefer it to the alternative—working with silent, passive, unadventurous kids. I would rather try to calm a fanatic than raise a corpse any day.

It's been my experience that the kid who is sharp enough to get into trouble is a person with enough creative energy to do something really significant. These group members are often most in need of discipline seasoned with praise.

Amy Carmichael, at the age of seventeen, began working with the poor children of Belfast. Later in her career, while working in India, she saved the lives of countless children meant to be sold as temple prostitutes and sacrifices. Elizabeth Elliott, in an article entitled "Amy Carmichael" (in *Heroes*, ed. Ann Spangler and Charles Turner [Ann Arbor, Mich.: Servant, 1990]), says this about Amy as a child:

> The eldest of seven children, she often led the rest of them in wild escapades, such as the time she suggested they all eat laburnum pods. She had been told the pods were poisonous, and thought it would be fun to see how long it would take them to die.

Or, take Brad for instance: He was one kid who was always giving us fits. He would be the one to take the clapper out of the camp bell, freeze the camp director's underwear in the freezer, or put goldfish in the camp pool. But I liked this kid. He was fun to be around, and I saw potential in him that others often times could not.

One October we did a haunted house, and I put Brad in charge of the "operating room." It was terrific! Brad put in extra hours after school securing large bones, medical equipment, and doctors' outfits. He was wonderful at organizing his crew. Everyone pointed out what a great job he had done. That haunted house completely changed Brad's attitude about himself. He began using his abilities for the Lord in other areas such as teaching the fourth-grade class. Brad is now married and is a successful entrepreneur running his own business. He is still a character, but he is now using his energy for the good of others.

A good way to motivate young people who have had behavior problems is to give them recognition when they start doing well. It is important to let young people know they are on target. Students need to know that you appreciate their efforts. Simple matter-of-fact feedback, if handled correctly, will not embarrass most high school students. It tells them that you recognize their mature and responsible attitudes and actions.

The need for recognition is one of the basic emotional needs of every human being. It's the drive that keeps us going and trying "to do better every time." We especially want praise from people who are important to us.

PRAISING IMPROVED BEHAVIOR

There is not a more meaningful motivator than praise. When former UCLA Coach John Wooden was asked how he motivated his basketball players, he said, "I try to catch them doing something right." This isn't easy to do in youth work! We have so many frustrations and expectations with regard to our young people that we forget to praise them when we catch them doing something right.

Positive reinforcement is the key to effective discipline. You can't change behavior using negative consequences. Negative consequences may stop behavior, but if you want to change behavior, you must use positive consequences. Verbal reinforcers are the most accessible vehicle you have to demonstrate that young people are behaving appropriately. Remember that all human beings need positive input. Hand in hand with positive verbal responses are nonverbal responses. A smile, a wink, a pat on the shoulder, or a positive gesture can clearly communicate your support for appropriate behavior.

Positive interactions take only a few seconds now and then throughout your time with your youth group, while negative interactions are often time-consuming, exhausting, and disruptive. It is much more productive to commend a young person for doing something right than it is to wait for misbehavior to get your attention.

Furthermore, the young people in your youth group shouldn't have to do something extraordinary to win your praise. If you praise effort and progress now, the big things will come later. Praise is particularly valuable for a young person who is doing his level best at something that is especially hard for him.

These days, most of the reminders young people hear focus on their problems. Kids hear about their mistakes from everyone. Think how much better off our young people would be if they heard positive reminders that, regardless of their failures, they are moving in the right direction.

It's been said that it takes eight compliments to make up for one criticism in a person's life. Our task is to be cheerleaders for our young people, supporting, affirming, and encouraging them. Sometimes what young people need is a good locker room pep talk.

Remember that effective praise must be sincere. Young people can spot phony praise or flattery in an instant. Be careful, however, not to praise something you don't like because, if the young person believes you, she'll go on doing that same thing until you wish you'd been more honest. That student will be like a small dog who keeps begging her master to throw a stick. Praise is like icing on a cake. Too much of it can be sickening; not enough of it makes the cake unappealing.

Look for intelligent, thoughtful questions asked by a student during a discussion. Keep your eyes peeled for a student putting someone else first—even if it's something small like a student leaving the last doughnut for somebody else. Listen for good deeds mentioned by others regarding activities away from the church setting, when no authority figures are watching.

By praising your young people for good things, you are unconsciously training yourself to concentrate on positive things. Unfortunately, many youth workers do the reverse. They are on the lookout for the wrong things their young people do and are ready to pounce on them.

EMPHASIZE PROGRESS

I do much better with my young people when I remind myself that being responsible is not natural. Responsibility is a social skill. Contrary to some youth workers' opinions, people do survive without being responsible. All of us would agree, however, that learning responsibility is desirable and leads to a better quality of life for everyone.

One of the things that helps me the most in allowing this learning to take place is to look at progress and not simply the finished product. Young people become excited when they know that you see them progressing in some good directions. Tell them and tell yourself that God is at work in their lives, and that you like what you see happening. Young people are more aware of their failures than we realize, and they are much less sure of their successes.

When I was in college, I was in a class led by a visiting professor from another college in town. He taught the entire semester. He would ask for comments on certain Bible passages, and I would raise my hand and give my insights from the previous night's studying. I had studied hard and wanted to make a good impression on this professor. His response caught me by surprise. He would not only disagree with an answer but would begin to belittle me in front of the rest of the class. He would comment on how no one with intelligence could possibly come up with an answer like mine. He also had a way of calling students he didn't like by their last names and students he liked by their first names. He would say to me, "Now let's hear what Mr. Christie has to say on this subject." Maybe he thought this would get me to study even harder, but I simply became so discouraged that I stopped going to the class. The thought of being made fun of in front of my peers was too great a threat to handle. I have always prayed that I would remember that experience as an example of how not to teach my own students.

Paul Hauck, in *How to Do What You Want to Do: The Art of Self-Discipline*, emphasizes *effort* instead of *achievement* as a measure of success:

> It is more important to *do* than to do *well*. The main difficulty people have who are driven by perfection is that they have a faulty definition of success. To them success is doing something 100 percent okay and hardly anything less. It simply does not make sense to define success as near perfection. Think of success rather as a slight bit of improvement over what you were able to do before. Even if you are trying something and do not see improvement, you are still entitled to say that you are improving, because the benefits of practice will show up later. As long as you are attempting something, improvement is being made. Even if

81

your performance goes down, as it sometimes will, you can still learn from the experience. And that is the name of the game.[19]

WAYS TO PRAISE

To get the most from your attempts to praise young people, try to offer praise as soon as possible—shortly after the desired behavior has been accomplished. The payoff should be as immediate as possible. This advice is based on the psychological fact that the faster the payoff is, the more powerful it is in strengthening the good behavior.

It's very important that your praise be specific. Use brief descriptive statements which tell young people what was worthy of comment. Vague feedback simply tells students that they did a nice job. This type of statement fails to communicate exactly what was worthy of comment. Nonspecific praise creates praise "junkies" who are never really satisfied. In order for young people to repeat their good behavior, they need to know specifically what they have done right!

One of the most common mistakes in providing positive feedback is to use a pet phrase over and over again. To see if you do this, you may want to bring a small tape recorder with you as you lead a Bible study or when you are around the youth group. If you notice the same phrase four or five times on one tape, it is being overused. If a phrase is overused, young people quit hearing it. This can be avoided by focusing on the use of specific, descriptive comments. If you want to, you can leave out comments which assign a value, such as *terrific, wonderful,* or *fantastic.*

DON'T EMBARRASS WITH PRAISE

Though verbal praise is an effective reward, it's also true that, in general, high schoolers do not like to be singled out in front of their peers. They get embarrassed. Some young people find it difficult to take direct positive reinforcement. Instead try praising these group members after a meeting or privately. Be creative! Write them notes, or if you announce someone's good deed to the group, do it in a humorous way. Don't be "gushy" or overdo it.

High schoolers can be embarrassed by positive feedback because they don't want to be singled out as a T.P. (Teachers Pet), or "Goody Good"—especially if the young person has cultivated a "tough guy" image. While some positive feedback can be given very naturally in front of the youth group, other comments will lose their power.

While flowery, emotional praise may embarrass high school young people, calm, quiet, matter-of-fact statements will give young people the recognition they need. Positive feedback should not imply that you are treating young people any differently from the way you would treat an adult.

It is natural to follow a positive comment to a young person with a pause. In interactions with other adults, this is the normal pattern: "Allison, I really like your new haircut." This statement would be followed by a pause, as you wait for the person to respond. However, using this same interaction pattern with a student in a youth meeting with others watching can cause problems. If you tell a young person that she has done a particularly nice job and then pause, she will feel she must respond. If she says something acceptable, she may worry that everyone will think she is "brownnosing." Instead, many young people will respond with embarrassment or with a wisecrack. If praise is followed by a pause, your comment may actually be punishing to a student.

This problem can be eliminated by giving positive feedback and then immediately shifting the focus to another topic or subject or young person. By shifting the focus from the one who has been praised, you eliminate the pressure that positive feedback potentially puts on young people.

Some young people feel uncomfortable with positive feedback because they have had so little. You may wish to meet privately with these kids and discuss ways that they can respond to positive comments. Every young person needs to have enough self-worth to accept recognition from someone else. In the same way, some youth workers don't know how to use or give praise, simply because they rarely received enough praise when they were teenagers.

You may encounter a few young people who misbehave immediately following a positive comment. These young people view themselves as troublemakers. Though they take pride in efforts noticed by a youth leader, they also tend to panic, thinking, "Now I'm expected to be perfect." Fear often leads this young person to misbehave, a way of saying, "I am the same problem teenager that I have always been." Misbehavior creates a safe environment. These young people need a lot of private feedback to motivate appropriate behavior. Minor misbehavior should not deter you from expecting and recognizing success in these young people.

A high school student may have had years and years of seeing himself as a loser. It will not be easy for him to give this up. Your positive expectations will be threatening, but wanted all the same.

BE SURE PRAISE IS DESERVED

When youth workers give praise and encouragement, there are two factors which must be remembered. I've stressed the fact that when a young person is overly criticized he will become discouraged. The other side of the coin is, if the young person is overly praised, it may have an equally bad effect. Lavish praise when it is unmerited not only loses its value as a reward and motivator, it is discouraging.

Constant praise is neither possible nor desirable. If you praise everything, regardless of whether it represents real achievement, effort, or progress by the young person, you may make her expect praise even when she doesn't deserve it. An exclusive diet of candy isn't good for anyone. But as long as you are sincere, it's better to overpraise than underpraise. This is doubly true when you feel that perhaps you haven't been using enough praise and are trying to teach yourself to take notice of and remark on a young person's effort and progress.

If the youth leader praises behavior that requires no effort, the young person is likely to be embarrassed because he won't feel he deserved the praise. He may feel he is being praised for babyish behavior, or that the youth leader is trying to con him into working hard. Be sure to give positive praise only when the young person has behaved in a way that is more mature than usual. This does not mean that only the highest performing young people get positive feedback. It means that every young person who tries to surpass his or her typical performance should get some recognition from the youth leader.

PRAISING THE TOTAL GROUP

Acknowledging the efforts of an entire group of young people helps establish a sense of cooperation and community within the youth group. Group recognition is also a comfortable way for high schoolers to accept praise and take pride in their accomplishments.

Group praise should be used frequently, but it also must be used carefully. Don't include the entire youth group if the entire youth group wasn't involved. Remember: praise must be earned. A good example might be, "I've noticed those that have been having personal quiet times have had a dramatic increase in sensitivity to others."

Avoid group praise that specifically excludes one or two individuals. It would be inappropriate to say, "All but two of the members of our youth group worked hard on this project." This does not serve as praise to the ones who worked—it only gives attention to the two people who did not. Group praise should be positive and communicate that all young people are expected to participate and do their best.

NOW ASK YOURSELF

1. Are you on your kids' team or on their backs most of the time? How would your kids see it?

2. Are there any pet phrases that you use repeatedly when praising young people? What are they, and what other phrases could you use?

3. Stop and write a brief note to compliment a young person who did something worthy of praise this last week.

4. Can you think of some funny items you can give out to recognize young people's achievements? I have given out old record albums that I've gotten at Salvation Army stores, barf bags from airlines, packets of hand soap from hotels, etc.

5. This Sunday, praise at least two young people—one publicly and one privately.

"I knew it was over when they put the 'Honk if you're horny' sticker on the bus. Or was it the whoopie cushion under the organist? Maybe it was when . . ."

CHAPTER 8

ANGER:
YOURS, MINE, AND THEIRS

It was happening again. As Joe Youthworker struggled on, trying to teach this week's Sunday School lesson to a class of rowdy ninth graders, he felt his anger building inside. "Hey, you guys, be quiet!" he said, for what felt like the hundredth time. A trio of especially rambunctious boys in the corner started to laugh.

Joe turned around to draw a simple chart on the chalkboard. A spitball came flying over his shoulder from the direction of the troublesome three in the corner. It splatted on the board, inches from Joe's head. Losing it, Joe spun around and hurled the chalk in the direction of the corner rowdies. "Don't try that again!" he yelled.

Then instant guilt set in. Once again his attempts at discipline had failed. Once again anger had taken control of Joe and his classroom. He wondered if it was time to get into another line of work.

I admit it. I've gotten angry with my youth group kids. Anger is a tough issue to deal with in the church. So I started looking at what makes youth leaders angry, what made Jesus angry, and what we can do to constructively deal with anger.

DON'T LET YOUR MOLEHILLS TURN INTO MOUNTAINS

All of us can identify with Joe Youthworker in one way or another. When discipline breaks down, it's easy to respond with anger and frustration. But here are a few tips to keep in mind to prevent molehills from growing into mountains of anger:

• Before taking "official action," count to 10. Better yet, try a 110. Don't do anything drastic until you listen a lot, think a lot, and pray a lot.

• Remember that a youth worker needs to be secure. If you don't feel secure, try to pinpoint your areas of insecurity and work on them. Don't let insecurity become an excuse for acting rashly or harshly. Some youth workers who feel insecure go out of their way to prove that they *are* in control. Afraid that their power is eroding, they're quick to make young people knuckle under. Teens need youth workers who serve as leaders and counselors, not as overlords.

• Before making any pronouncement on a request from kids, buy some time by saying something like, "Let me think about that." Give them a specific time when you will let them know your opinion. This will help you keep from giving a quick "yes" or "no" which might cause friction later.

• Work through your response to situations with adult sponsors or other youth workers. Get their help, advice, and prayer support. Double-teaming is an effective strategy in basketball and in youth work.

• Avoid arguments if at all possible. Don't spend your precious time in endless debate with students. When young people argue with you, keep repeating what behavior you desire from them and do not get sidetracked. By repeating what you want, you, rather than the students, stay in control. Don't allow discussions to turn into destructive arguments. Though some arguing is occasionally OK and necessary in communication, take a "time-out" if the argument becomes hostile or hurtful. Then come back to the issue at a later time.

REASONS LEADERS GET ANGRY

Why do youth leaders get so angry with their teenagers? Aren't we supposed to nurture them, love them, encourage them, lead them?

The more I think about it, the more I realize that most of *my* anger came from being bloated with high expectations. I'd read Ephesians 3:20: "Now to him who is able to do exceeding abundantly beyond all that we can ask or think." Therefore, I expected God to go so far beyond my expectations I thought I couldn't dream big enough for him. As a result, I was constantly dreaming big dreams that ended up on the ash heap. I became angry when the kids didn't perform as I expected.

Looking back on the years I've worked in youth ministry as a youth pastor, I realize my reason for becoming angry with my kids wasn't scriptural. My anger centered on the problem of my high expectations vs. their low-level responses—not what Jesus modeled as a reason for getting angry. So I went to God's Word. There I gained insight into the complicated emotion called anger.

REASONS JESUS GOT ANGRY

Using Jesus as a model for my actions, I discovered there actually are times when youth leaders ought to get angry with their young people. On at least three occasions, Jesus himself got angry. Here are his reasons:

• **Irreverence.** In John 2:13-22, we read about how Jesus drove the moneychangers out of the temple. He was incensed by their irreverence and their use of God for material gain.

• **Hypocrisy.** When Jesus was about to heal the man with the withered hand (Mark 3:1-6), the Pharisees condemned Him for healing on the Sabbath. In this case, hypocrisy and lack of compassion aroused His wrath. Besides all that, Jesus felt sorry for them.

• **Unbelief.** Jesus became angry with the cities of people who refused to believe in Him even though He showed them miracles (Matt. 11:20-24). Here, unbelief enraged Him.

Similarly, a youth leader has a right—even a responsibility—to confront teenagers who are irreverent, hypocritical, unloving and unwilling to believe in the face of overwhelming evidence. We are called to "be angry, yet not sin" (Eph. 4:26-27). That's the challenge. Leaders can express their anger, but shouldn't become violent, insulting, profane, or downgrading.

So how do leaders deal with anger in light of Scripture? There are constructive ways to deal with anger.

DEALING WITH OUR OWN FEELINGS OF ANGER

To cope with our own anger, we need to admit openly and accept graciously that anger is here to stay. A hundred thousand youth workers cannot be wrong; they have all gotten angry at their young people at some time. Our anger has a purpose; it shows our concern. Failure to get angry at certain moments indicates indifference, not love. Those who love cannot avoid anger. This does not mean our young people can withstand torrents of rage and floods of violence. It does mean that they can benefit from anger which says: "Enough is enough, there are limits to my tolerance."

When we start feeling irritated inside, but continue to be nice on the outside, we convey hypocrisy—not kindness. Instead of trying to hide our irritation, we can express it effectively. Anger, like a deep breath, cannot be held indefinitely. Sooner or later, we are bound to explode. When we lose our temper, we become temporarily insane. We become dangerous. We attack and insult. We say and do things to those we love that we would hesitate to inflict on a stranger. When the battle is over, we feel guilty and resolve never to lose our temper. But anger soon strikes again.

When feelings of anger are constantly stifled, both physical and mental health deteriorate. Anger is an energy that must find an outlet. If we deny ourselves an outlet, the same energy starts to consume us.

Instead of trying to suppress anger altogether, youth workers can express it in non-destructive ways. The expression of anger should bring some relief to the youth worker, some insight to the teenager, and no harmful aftereffects to either of them. In expressing anger, we consciously need to avoid creating waves of resentment and revenge. We want to get our point across and then let the storm subside.

Understanding your anger and expressing it in a healthy manner is crucial to your relationship with young people. It is important that you provide a role model showing teenagers how to handle anger. It is also important that you and your young people have a healthy give-and-take between you.

In dealing with your own angry feelings, adopt a style in which you try not to blame, attack, or insult the other person involved in the incident. Rather, when an incident occurs in which angry feelings are raised, try confronting the other person with an "I" statement, such as "Jeff, when you poke other students and make them react, I feel resentful and upset because I must stop my teaching to act as a referee." Such an "I" statement attempts to put the incident into perspective. It is a clear statement describing the upsetting behavior, how it makes you feel, and how it affects you. Such statements have the advantage of putting the focus on the disruptive behavior, while allowing the young person to become more aware of how his or her behavior affects others.

Another way to release general psychological tension is to engage in some physical

"*The junior highs say that they're really sorry and it won't happen again.*"

activity. Take a vigorous walk around the building. Such activity will provide you and the young person with an opportunity to release some energy and unwind.

On those occasions when you feel like exploding by "dumping" your anger on a young person, do so in writing. Take a few minutes at any time to write to the "offending" person about your angry feelings. Let it all come out. Don't save anything. Let the person know how furious he or she has made you feel. Be emotional; don't try to be logical. Once you have it all out on paper, fold it, address it, and then throw it away. (You might want to tear it up first!) You will be amazed at how successfully this technique tends to satisfy the need to express anger. Once the anger is expressed, you can then approach the problem with more rationality and less emotion.

Remember that there's often a vast difference between what God's will is and what we hope will happen in our young people's lives. But the more we understand human (and teenage) nature, the better we know God's plan, and the more we focus on *His* priorities, not ours, the more we'll be in tune with Him and will pick up the melody. Consider these suggestions for dealing with anger.

1. Study the Scriptures. Use the Bible to understand human nature, how God responds to it and how He transforms sinners to His likeness.

For instance, I often became angry at my youth group's uncaring attitude. Then I read the book of Jonah. On occasion, I tired of the emotional roller coaster teenagers ride—giving up one day, gung-ho the next. But I began studying people such as Moses and Elijah, who also slipped into the pits of discouragement at times.

As I looked at these people and saw how God dealt with them, I was stunned at how often He was patient, kind, and understanding, rather than angry. When we see young people as God sees them—sheep without a shepherd—we can begin to love them.

2. Find a loyal friend. Seek someone to help you gain perspective. If your expectations are too high, maybe an objective friend can help you become more realistic. The Lord tells us, "If any man lacks wisdom, let him ask of God" (James 1:5). Ask God to bring someone into your life who can listen, provide tactful counsel, and help you see as God sees.

3. Strive to understand teenagers. Knowing the psychology of the average teenager can help you understand why kids are apathetic and into "all the wrong things." It will also help you keep cool when they do things you don't like.

4. Stick to God's priorities. The longer I'm in youth ministry, the more I see the wisdom of Jesus' pouring His life into twelve men. I like to see the big splash; I love it when the church is jammed with kids craning their necks and smiling at a rally or concert. But the kids who last are the discipled ones.

A primary reason we get angry is because we're frustrated. But why do we get frustrated? Because we're focusing on our own priorities—not God's.

So when you find yourself getting angry at the kids under your leadership, ask yourself:

- Do I understand how God deals with struggling people?
- Are my expectations too high?
- Do I know what makes teenagers tick?

• Are my priorities in order?

When you focus on the things Jesus focused on, you get angry at the things He got angry about. But you also begin to love as He loved, lead as He led, and give as He gave.

WHEN YOU GET ANGRY

There are times when a youth leader gets angry at kids. That's the nature of this ministry. Think about what to do when you get angry. Be prepared with a strategy to deal with this emotion. Here are a few do's and don'ts:

Don't . . .
• use a sarcastic tone.
• use a put-down.
• quit.
• handle the problem in front of the whole group.
• get yourself into a power struggle.
• humiliate.
• ignore bad behavior.
• be surprised at bad behavior.
• tell other people about your private confrontation with the person who made you angry.

Do . . .
• admit your anger.
• use the person's name.
• ask the person to talk with you privately.
• speak firmly.
• insist that bad behavior stop.
• call off the activity if you're unable to deal with the bad behavior any other way.
• insist other adults help with discipline.
• train adults to deal with anger.
• train adults to move physically close to the person making trouble.
• conference with parents if you're unable to work out the problem.
• ask other youth leaders for advice.
• intervene immediately when violent behavior occurs.
• notice good behavior and tell the person.
• cool off briefly before you discuss the problem with the person.
• ask the person in private what the problem is.
• be specific about the behavior you object to.
• apologize if you're wrong.
• allow the person to save face.
• demonstrate Christian forgiveness.
• make it clear you expect good behavior.
• remind your group often that Christian groups are different from other groups.
• show the group you forgive the person who made you angry.

• share a prayer of thankfulness when the conflict is over and the problem resolved.

• ask the person what's an appropriate punishment or what course of action you should follow. (You don't have to do it, but the "misbehaver" often has a good idea that will take care of the situation.)

ABUSE OF AUTHORITY

Authority and control are important. They are a part of living. And they also have a place in your youth group. There are appropriate uses of authority and control. The trouble is that control is hard to turn off. The more we use it, the more we want to use it. It's like eating potato chips—once you start, it's hard to stop.

Because control is so easy to use, we are tempted to use it more often than we intend. As our young people grow up, instead of using less control and becoming more and more of an influence in their lives, we find ourselves hooked on using control, restraints, and manipulation. After all, we may rationalize, an authoritarian approach takes less time. Unfortunately, as a result, we no longer come across to our young people as caring and loving youth workers.

In discipline, it is important to set up special guards when emotionally exhausted. If I am angry at anyone, I may take it out on the youth group. This is particularly true if someone with authority over me has been wearing me thin. Too tired, too busy, too hurried; at times like these I can make serious mistakes. Read the tragic experience of Frederick McCarty, from *Growing Pains in the Classroom*, about a teacher whose sense of power (and possible exhaustion) cost him a student who had idolized him:

> Mr. G. was my favorite English teacher I loved the way he read Shakespeare. He had great "culture" in my eyes. I tried to be like him. When the other kids would cut him down in cafeteria discussion, I'd defend him vigorously. I tried to talk like he did and express opinions identical to his.
>
> One morning, we came into class, my friend and I, chatting about something or other and seated ourselves. As the bell rang, I finished my sentence and turned around. "McCarty, talking after the bell! For tomorrow you have a discipline assignment. Write a 300 word essay on "The Pleasures of Contemplation and Solitude."
>
> I blushed, embarrassed and angry. That night I sweated over the the essay. It had to be perfect for him, I knew. I was filled with a sense of betrayal, anger, and resentment. Our high school gave a minimum of four hours of homework each night. It was a crushing burden to me.
>
> The next day, Mr. G. ordered me to read the essay aloud. In the essay, I had discussed the beauty that Mankind, from Socrates to Sartre, had always found in contemplation and solitude and how this punishment assignment had interfered with my ability to contemplate!
>
> Mr. G. blushed and threw my paper in the trash can. "Now perhaps you'll be quiet after the bell," he said sarcastically. I was quiet in his class after that. Between bells I said nothing for the rest of the year. A gulf had opened between us. I did the minimum I could get away with in his class. I couldn't believe my former idol could be so petty and gratuitously mean."

Mr. G. thought he was teaching me respect for learning and for him. Instead he deepened my distrust, added to my resentment, cost me an idol, and limited my learning experience.[20]

WHEN YOUNG PEOPLE GET ANGRY

Children often store up a great deal of anger during their earlier years because they do not have adequate means of releasing feelings of frustration, confusion, and helplessness. Teenagers, however, have greater opportunity and ability to release these energy-charged feelings. Often they come out in the form of anger. The combined force of past anger and current anger sometimes causes teenagers to overreact.

Adolescent anger is often closely associated with the need to rebel or push away from parents and other authority figures. Energy from the anger is used to strengthen the pushing-away process. Angry reactions also express the youth's need to gain more of a sense of control over his or her life. These reactions, although uncomfortable and often scary to deal with, can be normal and healthy (unless destructively intense) when handled appropriately. But when mishandled, they can turn into rage, hostility, or resentment. Rage is anger that is so intense that it is beyond a person's control. Hostility is anger that is felt for a longer period of time and involves the wish or impulse to inflict pain or harm to the object of the anger. Resentment is another form of anger that develops when a hurt or transgression is not confronted and forgiven.

Haim Ginott, in his book *Between Parent and Teenager*, shares this insight:

> There is no way to win a war with our children. Time and energy are on their side. Even if we mobilize and win a battle, they can strike back with awesome vengeance. They can become defiant and delinquent, or passive and neurotic; they have all the weapons. If enraged enough, a teenage boy can steal a car and a teenage girl can get pregnant. They can worry us to death or put us to public shame.[21]

Don't try to win an argument with an extremely angry young person. You can't. They only get angrier. The young person needs to get the anger out before you can reason with him or her. They need to get it out in a way that will not cause any damage. Don't let them repress it, or it will simply go underground and build. Be thankful that they trust you enough to let you see them in this angry state. Try to have a neutral look as they pour all of their anger out. After the anger is out, they will be emotionally drained and more open to your input. Be sure to affirm them by telling them you were proud that they didn't take their anger out in more aggressive ways.

NOW ASK YOURSELF

1. How do you handle anger in your own life? What are some ways you can improve your ability to deal with difficult situations?

2. Make a list of positive ways to dispel anger.

3. How would you handle an extremely angry teenager?

GETTING RID OF DISTRACTIONS

Susie Youthworker was puzzled. She had worked very hard on today's Bible study lesson for the high school group. It was relevant, based on needs she knew her students had. She had a lot of energy, enthusiasm, and great visuals. But looking out across the dingy basement meeting room, she could tell she had lost her students. Most of them were slouched in their metal folding chairs with dazed expressions on their faces. A few, clustered in the back corner, were whispering to each other, though it was hard to tell who in the dim light. In the warm, quiet room, a feeling of sleepiness and apathy seemed to have settled down. Some of her own energy draining away, Susie wondered, *Where did I go wrong?*

Without knowing it, our friend Susie was close to figuring out the problem when she asked herself *where* she went wrong. In this case her problem was centered on *place* rather than content or presentation. Many discipline problems can be headed off at the pass if we stop to consider how physical environments affect learning and behavior.

Be sure to evaluate the layout of the room used by your young people. Allow students to make that room their own. They could paint the room and put in new carpet, for example, if your budget permits.

Each week or month put new posters on the walls. All young people will be distracted sometime during a lesson and their minds may begin to wander as they look around the room. The secret is to have things on the walls that relate to the topic of the day. Even if they do look around, they will still be getting the thrust of the message through other visual methods.

Cleanliness is also important in preventing discipline problems. I'm not talking about a hospital-white type of room, but we do want our young people to be proud of the room they meet in. Make sure it is light, bright, and well ventilated.

Church rooms are usually overheated, especially during the winter. Heat tends to make us sleepy and contributes to the lethargy that some teenagers naturally experience. You can alleviate the situation by merely opening a window or resetting the thermostat.

Church rooms can have too much or too little light. If your room has bright, harsh lighting, you can simply turn off some of the lights, or if they are on a timer switch, you can unscrew some of them. Bring more lights from home if your room is dim. Good lighting will help young people become more relaxed and receptive to learning.

Room dividers can create a variety of spaces for get-away zones, learning centers, preparation areas for skits, or for discussion groups. The only drawback is that they are not soundproof. With several discussion groups going at the same time in one room, the noise can be unbearable.

Arrange furniture to meet teaching and learning goals. If your goals call for group work, you may want to cluster chairs or tables. Your learning goal should determine the furniture arrangement rather than allowing the furniture arrangement to dictate the choice of learning goals.

The number of chairs in the room is also important. If you have a room set up with 500 chairs, and you know you are only going to have fifteen young people, you are asking for trouble. When the kids come into the room, it will look to them as though you were planning for a lot more people and that they made the wrong choice in coming to this meeting, because obviously 485 people went somewhere else! They will think they are missing out on something and will believe that, no matter what happens in that meeting, it can't be good because "no one is here."

The size of the room in which you meet is also important. If you have four kids in your youth group, don't meet in the main auditorium. Meet in a closet or rest room! Then when you get six kids coming, you can move into a larger room (maybe the custodian's office). Cramming into a small room has a great psychological effect on kids and it's also a lot of fun.

When speaking to your group, don't stand in front of a bright window, or your facial features become almost indistinguishable. Remember that kids need to see you if you want to keep their attention.

COPING WITH LATECOMERS

Does it drive you up the wall when half of your group comes into youth meeting just in time for the closing prayer? Every time a young person comes into the room late, everything stops as everyone stares at the latecomer. Most of the time these latecomers cannot just come in quietly and find a seat. No, they have to come in and make sure everyone knows they are now here so everything can begin.

Start with a "bang" to encourage promptness. Fight young people's tendency to be late by starting on time. Don't run after kids, scream or remind them what time it is. Instead, start each meeting with a quick, hilarious activity that'll grab their attention. Change the opener each time so kids never know what to expect. Eventually, they'll be hooked on your creativity.

Another possible way to eliminate this problem is to have a youth worker posted at the back door to escort the latecomer in quietly at an appropriate time in the program. Another suggestion is to lock them out. This approach may be controversial, so clear it with your church board and your parents. Warn the kids in advance that starting the next week, the doors will be locked five minutes after starting time, and no one else will be allowed in. Most of the kids won't believe you will do it. But stick to your guns, even if only a third of your group is there on time. However, I wouldn't do this every week—maybe once or twice a year.

The first time I pulled a "lock out," the kids in the room couldn't believe I was actually going to lock out the rest of the kids. They wondered what we were going to do with so many of our group left outside. We proceeded to have our Bible study with the few that were there on time. Then after our meeting, I told the kids in the room that they would have a lot of friends waiting outside in the parking lot who were probably pretty ticked off because they couldn't get into the meeting. I told the kids in the room that, when they got outside, they should tell their friends that it was the greatest meeting they had every been to—no matter what they really thought of the meeting! They did, and it was hilarious. The other kids were so mad they vowed they would arrive on time the next week.

In using this technique I remind our young people that Bible study is so important that I don't want them to miss a single minute.

GET TO YOUTH MEETINGS EARLY

Greeting young people at the door will demonstrate your interest in interacting with them from the moment they enter the youth group. Students feel secure knowing that they are in the right room and that the youth leader is ready for them. Your presence will also reduce the likelihood of misbehavior. If any young people try to enter your room rambunctiously or disruptively, you can take care of the inappropriate behavior outside the room.

HAVE VISUALS READY BEFORE YOUR MEETING

It is also important that you have all visuals ready before the meeting. If you teach junior highers, and you turn away from the class to write on the chalkboard and can't find the chalk, you may be in trouble. As you frantically look all over the floor for that missing piece of chalk, the kids are beginning to talk to each other, move around the room, throw paper airplanes, etc. It will take you another ten minutes to get their attention back—all because you didn't have chalk on hand when you started.

SHOWING FILMS

There are several things that can be done to prevent discipline problems from occurring when showing films in your youth group. Some of these tips also apply when you show videos.

1. Preview all films. Don't trust anyone's opinion of a film. There was one film that was recommended to me by some friends (and I use the term *friends* loosely). They said the film was about two guys who cross the Sahara desert on motorcycles and become Christians during their journey. Supposedly the producers were going to make this movie a secular film for a major studio but later decided to make a Christian film out of it. Without previewing it, I showed it to my kids one Sunday evening. It was the worst film I have ever seen.

Imagine these two guys riding what looked like Honda 50s across the desert. The first ten minutes of the film features the two motorcyclists going about 10 mph on a flat, straight stretch of desert. There is no dialogue, only the putt-putt-putt of the bikes. It was so boring I was dying!

It got worse. Evidently the motorcyclists had become Christians on their real-life journey. They had an accident and two missionaries had assisted them and introduced them to the Lord. Of course, they did not have their cameras rolling when the accident happened, so they had to fake it. Remember the old television program *Laugh-in* where the man rides his tricycle into the tree and falls over? You got it. These guys gently fall over with their bikes and then smile into the camera. The missionaries appear from nowhere in the middle of the desert. He is wearing a suit and she is wearing a dress with high heels. It was incredible. My kids were laughing so hard they were falling on the floor! I stopped the film and never did see how it ended. So much for great moments in youth ministry.

2. Make sure the sound is set at the correct volume. It's embarrassing to be eight minutes into a film and discover that the sound is not on. The opposite mistake is to set the volume too high. The kids are quiet with anticipation, so when the film comes on too loud, it even knocks high schoolers out of their seats.

3. Make sure the focus is set. If it isn't, your kids will yell out "Focus!" and then begin laughing.

4. Skip the countdown. If you don't skip the countdown in the beginning of the film, you know what your kids will do. They will start counting down: 5 . . . 4 . . . 3 . . . 2 . . . 1 . . . Kaboom! Forget about keeping a serious mood when this happens.

5. Clean the projector gate. Ever watch a film with a hair hanging down in front of the lens projector? It always seems to hang down in the oddest places. Your kids will be laughing as they see it in someone's ear or hanging from some building. This all can be eliminated by simply taking a clean cloth and cleaning the gate where the film winds through the projector.

6. Order the film in advance. It's embarrassing to announce a film and advertise it, only to have it fail to arrive on time because it was only ordered the day before. I have a friend who did this, and he had 2,300 high school kids in an auditorium waiting to see a 90-minute film which did not arrive. You'd better have a plan "B" or you will be in a lot of trouble.

7. Don't be in a hurry to turn the lights on. After a particularly moving film where half of your kids are crying, don't rush to turn on all the lights. The kids are dabbing their tears and are embarrassed. Leave the lights out and discuss the film in the quiet darkness.

GET EVERYONE'S ATTENTION BEFORE YOU START TEACHING

Always wait to get everyone's attention before you begin teaching. If you start teaching while some young people are still talking or are out of their seats, students will assume it's OK to engage in those behaviors while youth group is in session. Make waiting a habit, and give directions or start activities only when you have the group's attention.

You may discover that a little time spent eliminating potential distractions will pay off by eliminating the need for some discipline.

CONVICTION

The human spirit is attracted to conviction. It's repelled by halfheartedness. Often, kids who say their youth group is "boring" or "too serious" are really saying the group lacks conviction.

Conviction is more than enthusiasm or simple belief. It's living passionately for what you believe.

CONFIDENCE

Dogs sense fear, and so do teenagers! Confidence is a key to capturing and keeping kids' attention during "serious" activities. But confidence isn't the same as cockiness. Confidence means you're well-prepared, secure, humble and honest. When kids don't want to be serious, your confidence will help draw them in.

NOW ASK YOURSELF

1. Is the room you meet in conducive to learning? How can the physical environment of the room be improved?

2. Evaluate the success of the last film or video you showed your group. What went wrong? What went right? How can you improve response?

3. What procedure do you plan to use with latecomers in the future?

"Nope, the kids were no trouble at all."

SPECIFIC DISCIPLINE METHODS

This chapter offers you a smorgasbord of advice—a variety of disciplinary methods to deal with a variety of situations. Feel free to mix and match these approaches to meet the needs of your own group.

START OFF WITH CONTROL

Youth workers want to be liked, so the tendency is to be lax when it comes to discipline, at first letting kids get away with anything. In fact, it is much harder to add rules later on. It is far better to start off with more control in the beginning and loosen up a bit later. The problem many youth workers have is saying "no" to kids. It is probably the most difficult word to say in the English language because so few of us use it. Jesus said "no" to many people in a variety of situations:

HUMAN REQUESTS
Let me bury my father before I follow You.
(Matt. 8:21-22)

Tell my sister to help me with housework.
(Luke 10:38-42)

Stay in our town a little longer.
(Luke 4:42-44)

FRIENDS WHO ASKED FAVORS
Give my sons a privileged place next to You.
(Matt. 20:20-23)

Stop talking about Your death like that.
(Mark 8:31-38)

Tell us when the last things will occur.
(Acts 1:6-7)

Call down fire and destroy towns that reject You.
(Luke 9:54-56)

DEMANDS OF THE CROWDS
Work a sign for us here and now.
(Matt. 12:38-45)

Do here in Your own town the things we have
heard You did in Capernaum.
(Luke 4:23-24)

Give us the bread You gave us yesterday.
(John 6:41-58)

COMMON SENSE, LAW-AND-ORDER, CITIZENS' REQUESTS
Send the crowd away; they're getting hungry.
(Luke 9:12-17)

Keep this crowd quiet.
(Luke 19:37-40)

Make Your followers fast like John the Baptist does.
(Mark 2:18-22)

Answer the accusations against You.
(Mark 15:4-5)

Rev. George Niedeauer, "When Jesus Said No," *The Priest*
(December, 1978).

RECOGNIZE INDIVIDUAL PROBLEMS

Remember that the *entire* youth group is never at fault when things go wrong. At times it may seem like everyone is acting up, but in reality it is usually just two or three young people. If you can control these two or three, you can control the entire group. It's incredible how one young person by himself will be great; but then a certain chemistry takes place when a group gets together, and everything goes up for grabs. Get to know individuals that make up the group instead of treating the group as one.

BE A GOOD LISTENER

As youth leaders, we expect young people to listen to us, but all too frequently we don't take the time to listen to them. When someone important to us does not listen to our concerns, we begin to feel that we must not be worth much; we feel discounted. This can be especially true of young people, whose lives are a series of confusing changes. They need to know that their youth workers will listen to those things that are important to them. The youth worker who responds to a student's concerns with statements like "We can't take the time now to talk about that," or "That's off the subject," is probably making the student feel put down or put off.

Real listening does not necessarily mean agreement. It does involve clarifying and understanding another person's feelings and point of view.

Part of the difficulty with listening is that we must attend to far more than the spoken words, since nonverbal messages actually carry more weight than words. Look at the posture of the other person as they speak, and watch their gestures. We need to hear the feeling or the mood behind the speaker's words. As a listener, you must communicate in a nonverbal way that you are accepting, that you are nonjudgmental, that you are nonevaluating. Remember that your body language acts out what you are feeling.

Body language that is inappropriate for a listener:
- Turning your back to the person who is speaking
- Drumming your fingers on a table or chair while a person is speaking to you
- Not maintaining eye contact with the person who is speaking
- Yawning while a person is speaking to you
- Rummaging through a drawer or cupboard—or otherwise moving around while a person is speaking to you
- Checking your wristwatch or a clock while a person is speaking to you
- Carrying on another conversation while a person is speaking to you

As the listener, you must be accepting of the individual. This does not mean that you accept the situation, only the person. As the listener, you must take the time and the interest to listen.

Hope they feel free to express their thoughts and feelings. Set limits on *behavior*, not on *opinions*. A free expression of opinion, with proper rules of courtesy, is one of the healthiest goals a youth group can work toward. The effort will create an atmosphere in which people learn to listen to one another.

DON'T EXPECT TO BE POPULAR

When youth workers complain that they can't control their young people, I frequently ask the question, "Do they do what you ask them to do?" The answer is often, "Yeah, they do it, but I don't like the *way* they do it. It's their attitude, you see." When I pursue the issue, I find that youth workers often believe that teens should not only be compliant, but should also be delighted over the opportunity to comply.

But teenagers are not always happy about being corrected—a lesson we all learn eventually. Once at camp, we had a rule that no smoking was allowed the entire week at camp. One of the counselors noticed a new kid at camp lighting up during free time. The counselor went to the young person and explained the rule and asked the camper to put out the cigarette. The camper complied, but the counselor was upset and became uptight because the student didn't look thrilled at being told to put out the cigarette and warned that he would not be able to smoke all week. Instead of getting bent out of shape, the counselor should have been grateful that the camper was complying with his wishes. It may have been difficult for this kid to give up smoking for the week. After all, he had not internalized the counselor's opinion on the value of cigarette smoking (or lack of it).

Simply because you want a young person to stop doing something does not mean that she will no longer have that desire. Don't hassle a kid if she complies but is not happy about it. I'm not saying to accept back talk or any nastiness on the camper's part, but if the kid simply has an expression on her face saying, "This is a dumb rule," don't declare war right then and there. And don't try to convince her immediately what a great rule it is. I would, however, explain the reason for the rule at a later time when the person is ready to talk.

FORGIVE AND FORGET

Dredging up past mistakes for review is bad business, anytime and anywhere. Whatever discipline has been dished out previously, *forget it.* The behavior, the situation, what's happening or not happening may be criticized, but remember that your message should only concern the present behavior or situation. Don't use this opportunity to throw everything but the kitchen sink into your message.

Warren W. Wiersbe shares this memory from his family:

> If I err, I want to err on the side of forgiveness. There were probably times when I should have walloped the kids. Only now I am finding out things they did I never knew before—by listening to my son preach! He'll tell a story from his teens and I'll say, "I didn't know about that." But they seemed to have come through.
>
> On the other hand there were times when we disciplined the kids for things they didn't do. I discovered the truth later. Fortunately, where there's love, openness, honesty, and fun, kids somehow survive those injustices. Oh—a sense of humor really helps![22]

DON'T BORE KIDS WITH THE BIBLE

Jim Rayburn, founder of Young Life, said it years ago, and we've yet to improve on his insights: "It is a sin to bore kids with the Bible." It is far too important a book for us to merely mumble our way through a Bible study in an unprepared manner.

I wouldn't dream of going on a retreat without having every logistical detail covered, but I am amazed at how often I will stand up to speak with hardly any preparation and just "wing it." I have also noticed an interesting phenomenon: the less prepared I am, the grouchier I get.

One of the great communicators in Scripture (next to Jesus) is Apollos in Acts 18. He knew his stuff, and his content was class A. He was a communicator and he had done his homework. He was not a sloppy speaker; he spoke with exactness.

Kids need to see the Word of God as active, sharp, and exciting. In China they stand up if you are boring. In the middle of your talk—if you are not cutting it—the Chinese will simply stand up and wait for you to get your act together. Can you imagine your kids doing that in your meeting? Talk about intimidating! Earn your kids' respect by coming prepared.

ISOLATING A STUDENT

When young people seem unable to control their behavior, isolation can be an effective consequence. A short period of isolation is a safe and effective way of handling any situation where a student is emotionally upset. It gives everyone a breather. It often removes the young person from the cause of his trouble. He can be asked to step outside the classroom with another adult sponsor until you can get out to talk with him, or sent to a higher authority (youth minister, senior minister, elder, etc.), and go to an office with a sponsor until a meeting can be arranged. The only drawback to sending a student away is that the student's perception may be, "The youth leader doesn't know what to do with me, so he is getting rid of me." Only as a last resort should a person be separated from the group.

The positive effect is that many times when a young person is sent outside the room for misbehavior, it communicates that not being involved in an activity is a *punishment*, and therefore, the room must be a great place to be. So more students behave so that they can participate.

After the meeting, as you are talking to a young person who has caused a disturbance, use the eye/name/touch/gesture method. Get the person to look at you. Then call him or her by name. Touch the person gently on the shoulder, and then gesture with your other hand as you describe what happened and the reason he or she is outside the room. Explain how the person contributed to the problem. Share what you are trying to accomplish in the youth group and ask for help. Let the offender know you are personally hurt. Reflect grief through your facial expressions. Then close with prayer. Pray that at the next meeting you hope the things discussed there will meet the student's needs. Emphasize that you see this person as a valuable asset to the youth group.

A bad idea is to make a punishment out of something like having to go to lunch with you. Don't make it sound like having to spend time with you is a terrible thing.

Another form of isolation is to separate two young people that are constantly fighting. Either have someone sit between them or, as they walk in the room, suggest that they do not sit by each other. The crazy thing is that most rowdy kids have this built-in magnet that attracts them to other rowdy kids. Another possibility is to have one of the youth workers sit by a kid who might possibly be a challenge, without letting the student know why they are sitting near him.

IGNORING

Ignoring is a possible strategy for teaching a young person to behave in a more mature and responsible manner. When ignoring is selected as a consequence to misbehavior, the young person is being told that some behaviors are so childish, they are not worthy of a response. When you've told the student a certain behavior is annoying and unacceptable, and he or she continues the behavior, sometimes the best thing to do is ignore the young person. Instead of giving attention, take away the positive reinforcement. Be sure students don't get the wrong idea—that you are condoning misbehavior by ignoring it.

When the misbehaving young person behaves acceptably, interact with him. Demonstrate that you will ignore him only when he acts immaturely. As soon as the young person behaves as expected, he is a contributing member of the youth group.

TAPE-RECORD BEHAVIOR

Tape your times with the kids if you are having difficulty. Place the tape recorder in an unobtrusive spot. If your young people are likely to see what you are doing, tell them you are taping the class to improve your teaching.

The recorder should be turned on for the class period. Students will usually cease disrupting when the recorder is turned on, which is, of course, one of the goals of this technique. It will also give you a chance to evaluate your teaching as you listen to yourself interact with your youth group.

STOP SPEAKING

I've found that the best thing to do is to simply stop speaking until everyone is listening. Even if I'm midsentence, I stop. This is an effective way to let kids know that your lesson or activity is important—it shouldn't have to compete with anything else. This works!

When kids get unruly, simply quietly look at them with an expressionless face. And wait. Usually this technique results in silence within a few seconds. If it takes longer, I'll say something like, "We'll begin when everyone's ready to listen." If the problem is severe, I'll pull a chair out front and sit down. Inevitably, the kids tell one another to be quiet. It's positive peer pressure.

Here's why I believe this approach is best for most situations:

• Kids realize on their own the inappropriateness of talking when someone else has the floor. Through their own decision to settle down, they're learning how to act in a group.

• This approach leaves kids' dignity intact. No one is yelled at or belittled.

• Kids learn to police each other. The discomfort of watching a leader silently stare at the group provokes many kids to say, "Shhhhh!"

• This approach says: "I respect you as people, but I won't battle you for the right to be heard. You decide if the group would benefit from quieting down."

DISTRACTION LOANS

Occasionally young people will bring things to youth meetings that are distracting. When a demand is made with a high schooler to "hand that over," the pressure is on the young person to fire back a retaliatory remark. To ease the tension, it is far better to ask them to "loan" you the item for the hour or day or week—depending on where you are. Some of these items include hats that are tossed around the room, knives that are being shown off, pet snakes, mice, or lizards.

As you confiscate something, focus on the item, not the young person. You may want to make it humorous to ease the tension. Give the item a suspension. Talk to the item and scold it. In confiscating a nerf football that has been thrown around the room say, "I can't believe you did that! You've never acted this way before." The kids laugh, the problem is solved, and you can move on to more important things.

UTILIZATION METHOD

If you have a hyper teenager who cannot sit still, give him something to do. I'm not talking about putting him in a leadership position to straighten him out. That only backfires.

But you can involve the student in passing out or collecting papers. Keep him busy and involved without drawing attention to him, and many times the problem will be solved.

NEVER PUBLICLY EMBARRASS A TEENAGER

This is a tempting option. If you've spent hours preparing a lesson, the last thing you want is a disruption in the group. But before you embarrass a troublemaker, consider the consequences.

Teenagers are incredibly self-conscious. Your remark may stop the trouble-making behavior, but the resulting embarrassment could cost you a group member. And that one embarrassed teenager will probably tell five or six friends about what you did. Now you've lost them too. Most outbursts are designed to get your attention. You reward troublemakers when you stop everything to focus on them.

SILENT SPEAKING

If two or three young people in the back of the room begin talking as you are speaking to the entire group, continue moving your mouth as if you are talking, but don't let any words come out of your lips. It will get deadly silent in the room as all of the group members wonder if they are going deaf! However, the two or three that are talking will now suddenly sound extremely loud. They will look up and realize they are talking and stop. Then you can continue as usual and no one is particularly embarrassed.

Sometimes all you need to do with young people that are not paying attention is to give them eye contact. Look at them as you are talking until you get their attention and communicate with your eyes that you need their attention.

MOVE AROUND THE ROOM

You may have noticed that many of your rowdy young people tend to sit in the back of the room. Why not take your podium and move it to the back of the room after everyone is seated? The students in the back begin to panic. Each time, speak from another part of the room. As the rowdy young people enter the room they won't know where to sit because they will not know where you will be standing as you speak.

ELIMINATE SWEET TREATS

Youth groups are able to significantly lower the number of disruptive occurrences by eliminating all sweets from their youth meetings. Many youth groups are using foods that contain high nutrition but low levels of stimulants, even to the point of replacing candy at the camp store with fruit.

NEVER THREATEN WHAT YOU CANNOT OR WILL NOT DO

After trying every imaginable method to get your group quiet, have you ever gotten so mad that you finally yelled out a threat so idiotic that they knew you would never follow through on it? Something similar to, "If you kids don't shut up, I'll never allow you to go on another church activity as long as you live!" They may stop the noise for a second, until they realize you would never do such a thing. Impossible threats don't help at all. In fact, empty threats make things worse because the kids now know they have you!

When the freshmen enter our high school group each year, most of them are intimidated by virtue of being the youngest ones in the group. What I do each year breaks the ice and helps the freshmen get a glimpse of one aspect of our discipline methods. As all the young people in our high school group are coming in the room for Sunday School, they are talking and having a great time. I start trying to get them quiet, but I don't try very hard. Then I act like I am getting mad and finally yell out, "If you kids don't shut up, I'm going to rip your arms off!"

Well, it gets deadly silent except for one eleventh-grader in the front row who continues to talk loudly. I now walk directly to that student and repeat, "I told you—if you don't shut up, I'm going to rip your arms off." At this point you can hear a pin drop in the room. Every eye is on me and this one young person. It is deadly silent. I now reach over and grab one of his arms. (Now, what the other young people don't know is that I got together with this eleventh-grader before the meeting and fixed him up with a mannequin's arm up his sleeve.) After I grab the arm, I yank it right out. The freshmen kids in the back are screaming, "He did it! He really did it!" Then the kids realize we were kidding and everybody has a good laugh. Then I explain that whatever we say we are going to do in this youth group, they can bet we will follow through on it.

One problem I keep hearing about as I speak around the country involves kids who are late getting back to the church van or bus when an activity ends. Everyone is in the bus but one or two kids, and everyone leaves late because somebody had to take one last stroll around the camp. The bus then gets back to the church late, met by fifty angry parents who have been waiting forty-five minutes for the bus to arrive.

This used to happen to me, but it doesn't happen anymore. I now let parents know that if their kids are late getting back to the bus, I will call the parents, and it will be the parents' responsibility to drive to our location and pick up their kid who will be left behind. I warn the kids in advance that this is the policy and repeat the time they are to be at the bus at least four times.

I had to enforce this rule at our summer camp a couple of years ago. The caretaker of the camp was there at the time, so I knew the missing students would be safe. The parents had to drive the two-hour journey up the mountain to get their kids. They *were* mad, but I would rather have two parents mad at me than fifty. The word soon spread through the youth group that when Les says to be at the bus at three, you had *better* be there at three. Now obviously, there are certain situations where it would be harmful to leave a young person, so be selective about activities where you use this consequence.

FOLLOW UP

Follow up the person you've disciplined a few days after the incident. Don't let distance grow between you and trouble-makers. A good policy is to follow up every person you discipline two days later. Too often problem kids hear from adults only when they're in trouble; our rowdies need extra attention, especially when they are not being rowdy. Compensate for any disciplinary action with positive attention.

NOW ASK YOURSELF

1. Think of a situation in which you could have been a better listener. What went wrong?

2. Do you struggle with the desire to be popular with your kids? How does this hinder your discipline with them?

3. How can you make Bible study or Sunday School lessons more interesting?

4. What are you communicating to young people nonverbally?

5. Do you set limits on behavior and not on opinions? Do your young people feel comfortable talking to you about anything? How can you make yourself more accessible and create an atmosphere where questions and opinions are encouraged?

6. Are you a forgiving person? Remember the story of the unmerciful servant (owed millions, would not forgive the guy who owed him a few dollars)? Who are you in the story?

SECTION TWO

Sunday School Teacher Tom Dreams On...

DEALING WITH SPECIALIZED PROBLEMS

• Mary is often teased by the other kids in the group. She's overweight and all too often forgets to comb her hair or put on deodorant. She'll sit quietly and listen, but you often wonder if you really have her attention. When the other kids make fun of her, she lashes out with hostility, and then becomes withdrawn. You hate to come down hard on Mary because of her fragile self-image.

• Randy is also quiet and withdrawn, but his is an aggressive silence—the kind that dares you to try to break through his tough exterior. Some of the kids in the group refer to him as "wasted" and "fried," and you've talked to Randy's mother about her son's past history of drug and alcohol abuse. A year ago Randy went in for special treatment, and supposedly since then he has cleaned up his act. But you sometimes wonder if he's got everybody fooled and is really back into his old habits. Your efforts to get Randy involved always meet with resistance.

• Sharon can be a real pain in group settings. She never takes anything seriously and spends most of her time giggling and talking with her girlfriends, or else flirting with the guys in the group. But you are worried about her behavior outside the church, strongly suspecting she's involved in sexual relationships. When you try to discipline her in private or get her attention in Sunday School class, she just rolls her eyes as if to say, "Who cares?"

• Mike drives you up the wall. He drives the other kids up the wall too, with his hyperactive behavior, nonstop talking, practical jokes, and immature action. You know he has needed a father figure since his parents' divorce, but often your patience runs out as he tests your limits time and again. Mike is more than merely active or rowdy. He has no regard for rules of any sort and has already had minor run-ins with the law for shoplifting, being caught with alcohol, and drag racing late at night. How can you discipline a kid like this?

Mary, Randy, Sharon, and Mike are all examples of high-risk young people. They are usually the ones who are in trouble, or most likely to get into trouble. Chances of their success in the future are low; they have the same problems in school and at home that they do in the church. They are candidates for depression, suicide, drug addiction, social isolation, and teen pregnancy. Most of them come from difficult family situations where parents are too busy struggling with their own problems to cope with those of their kids.

Discipline for high-risk young people requires the kind of one-on-one attention that will really make a difference. The high-risk young person will need one special person who takes the time to support and encourage small successes. Of course, you can't provide this amount of time to everyone. One alternative is to have a church-wide support team that pairs one church member with one high-risk student. The support person will keep in touch with the young person to see how he or she is doing, make parental contacts, disciple, motivate, and encourage the young person.

Each church will need to set up its program for salvaging high-risk young people with the recognition that it cannot help every young person. However, if twenty church members work with twenty high-risk young people and only half are successful, at least ten young people will have learned that they can be part of a system that cares. For an individual, a high-risk program may mean the difference between living successfully in society or being another person on the fringes—in jail, on the streets, or living on welfare.

In addition to dealing with high-risk students, you're familiar with a number of other specialized problems in the youth group setting. This chapter deals with the do's and don'ts of handling those problems.

CRITICISM AND NAME-CALLING

Two approaches to avoid when handling special problems involve the use of criticism and name-calling. These two provide double-barreled destruction in your group.

If you could find a recipe for a happy youth group, it would call for just a pinch of constructive criticism. Unfortunately, many youth groups today shovel it out by the truckload. Here are some helpful hints on using constructive criticism. Never criticize the *person*. Criticizing the person lowers that person's self-esteem and feelings of self-worth. Separate the behavior from the person.

Remember, for every negative remark, it takes eight positive comments to make up for it. This includes critical comments that are intended to be constructive. Be sensitive to the individual. Select a time to share your insights with the young person when he is not surrounded by his peers, when both of you are not rushed, and after you have taken time to gain his respect.

Maybe a young person has a physical problem in the area of hygiene and you know the other kids are avoiding the one with the body odor. This problem needs to be pointed out to the young person, but do it gently—not with a condemning attitude, but as a friend. Constructive criticism not only points out the problem, but also offers practical solutions. Destructive criticism merely destroys the individual by pointing out the difficulty, leaving them an emotional wreck with no notion of a way of escape.

No matter what happens, don't resort to name-calling. Every teenager has some imperfections about which he is overly sensitive. The world usually takes notice of them to tease and ridicule. If a teenager is small, he will be called "shorty," "squirt," "shrimp," or "runt." If he is thin and tall, he is "beanpole," "stick," or "stretch." If he is fat, he will be named "fatso," "chubby," or "blimp." If he is weak, he may be called "sissy," "wimp," or "chicken." If he is uncoordinated he is called "nerd," "dork," "turkey," "geek," "jerk-n-a-half," "dip," or "dweeb."

Young teens suffer deeply from such nicknames, even when they pretend indifference. It is best that youth workers not tease their young people, even in jest. Insults cut deeper and last longer when they come from a youth worker. We can learn to communicate without sarcasm and ridicule. There is no place for biting comments in conversations between youth workers and young people. Sarcasm evokes hatred and provokes counterattacks.

Criticism of personality and character gives a young person negative feelings about herself. Abusive adjectives attached to personality have a devastating effect. When we call a young person "stupid" or "clumsy" or "ugly," there are reactions in her body and soul. She reacts with resentment, anger, and revenge fantasies.

A young person who is repeatedly made to feel stupid accepts such evaluation as fact. She may give up intellectual pursuits to escape ridicule. Since competition means failure, her safety depends on not trying.

WHEN A GROUP MEMBER DESTROYS PROPERTY

Require young people to repair, clean up, or pay for the damage they have done—and more. For instance, if a young person writes on a wall, he should be required to wash all the walls in the room. If a student sticks gum under her chair, she should be required to scrape off all the gum in the room. If a kid breaks a window, he should pay for it. The young person will have to work out a way to pay back any damages. They can be paid back in cash, or the expense for repairs can be worked off—perhaps earning $5.00 an hour by doing work around the church.

TEASING

If a young lady (or young man) in your group is having difficulty with other young people teasing her, emphasize that you cannot make the other kids stop teasing her by punishing them. Make it clear that the youth leaders understand her frustrations, but the only thing that will effectively stop the teasing will be her changing her own reactions. The easiest and most effective way to eliminate chronic teasing is for the victim to completely ignore it. Explain that immature young people will tease her to see her reaction. After all, it isn't fun to tease someone unless you get a reaction; that's the whole point of teasing. Point out that when she reacts to teasing, she is rewarding her tormentors.

Have the young person make a list of any names or comments that have bothered her. Go through the list and tell her what you would do to ignore them in each instance. Do some role playing with her, demonstrating how to respond properly. Begin with the names and comments that bother her the least. Do the role playing only if the young person wants to participate.

Young people learn to ignore teasing or to laugh it off when they have a good self-concept. In addition to learning to ignore teasing, the young person also needs help in building self-confidence.

USING EXCUSES

A young person who always has excuses feels that she can avoid being accountable for her own behavior. In the past, she probably managed to get out of work and avoid negative consequences for her actions. Since the strategy has been effective, making excuses has become a habit. This habit may have begun innocently, but the young person has become an unreliable person.

Young people who constantly make up excuses may also be young people who need attention. While making excuses, they receive a lot of immediate and individual attention. Some young people know how to manipulate a lot of adult time.

Your response will vary depending on the young person. A mild verbal reprimand should be used with young people who are unaware of their behavior. It should be used with young people who are likely to improve if they can learn to identify when their responses are inappropriate.

If a young person seems to need attention, ignoring the excuses is the most effective strategy for responding to excuses. The student must learn that giving excuses will not earn your attention.

Select a neutral time to discuss the problem with the young person. Explain that you would really like to trust the student but you are having difficulty knowing when to believe her.

SWEARING

Young people frequently swear because swearing is a part of their language environment. If young people have parents or peers who swear, swearing becomes a natural part of their language. It becomes a habit, much like saying "you know." Other young people begin swearing because they think it makes them appear more sophisticated, more mature, or tough.

Some young people swear to antagonize adults. Their intent is to get an emotional response from an authority figure. In this case, swearing becomes an attention-getter.

At a neutral time, explain to your youth group that you are concerned about the amount of swearing you hear. Explain that swearing is not appropriate and is offensive to many people. Warn them that some people will judge them solely on the basis of their language. Ask students to refrain from using bad language in your youth group.

If the problem persists, talk to individual students who are involved. Explain the consequences if the swearing continues. Give them some examples of exclamations that would be acceptable. Praise each student as he or she makes progress on breaking this habit.

Now Ask Yourself

1. How are you ministering to the "high-risk" young people in your group?

2. Have you ever employed criticism or name-calling? What was the result?

3. How do your small group discussions rate? How can you improve them?

©1990 Dan Pegoda

CAUSTIC KIDS

Like most youth ministers, I've been burned and burned again by troublemaking kids. Caustic-kid ministry is rarely fun. The word "caustic" comes from the word "cauterize," which is a medical term meaning to burn until you close off a wound. Caustic kids are kids who have burned peers and those in authority over them to the point where they have closed off almost all relationships. These are difficult kids to work with.

The tendency is to want to pull in the welcome mat. These are hardened kids. They are difficult to love. They may be in trouble with the law. What I have discovered over the years, however, is that many of these kids are like Tootsie Pops. You know, those little round candies on the end of a stick. They are hard on the outside, but once you get past that hard outer shell there is something soft and good in the center. Caustic kids are like that. Once you get past the calloused, hard veneer that covers them, there is a wonderful kid on the inside that just needs to be loved and to get out from behind that hardened exterior.

If you're one who shies away from disagreeable kids, I don't blame you. They're hard to love. It's natural for you to distance yourself from them. They give you every reason to not like them.

1. Caustic kids tend to be self-centered. They don't have winsome personalities. Often they're not even pleasant. They share a "gift" for repulsing people.

2. They don't respect you or your position. Caustic kids refuse to cooperate with you. They interrupt you with snide remarks. They undermine your authority by breaking rules. They try their best to lag behind and not participate.

3. They defy you at every step. Their icy stares grate on you. They couldn't care less about your ministry with the youth group.

4. They sabotage your ministry. Disagreeable kids talk against you to kids you're trying to reach. They tell their parents, and anyone who listens, lies about you.

5. They don't honor the effort you put into your work. Caustic kids call the youth programs boring, and they're not shy about criticizing with other kids.

6. They place your job in jeopardy. They can be the explosive catalysts that jeopardize your relationships with parents, other youth leaders, other teenagers, your senior pastor, and the church board.

7. They're a threat to your "success ratio." Your inability to break through caustic kids' rough exteriors can lead others to think you don't know how to handle difficult cases. They're a nagging reminder that you may not be as outstanding as you'd hoped.

8. They're a living illustration of what you're trying to keep your kids from becoming. Caustic kids love to look and act like they're from "the wrong crowd." They tell magnetic stories about parties they've gone to, movies they've seen, classes they've cut, and joy rides they've taken in stolen cars.

9. They're an ever-present irritant. Caustic kids bring the worst kind of music along on the church bus. They tune out everyone as they retreat beneath their headphones. They sneak off to smoke cigarettes . . . or worse.

10. They conflict with you because like forces repel each other. Youth leaders are characteristically strong-willed. Sparks fly!

Once nitric acid was used to determine whether an ore was real gold or fool's gold. If the mineral passed "the acid test," it was gold. The same is true for caustic kids. They test the purity and truth of your ministry with their "acid" behavior.

Though caustic kids offer plenty of reasons to pull in your welcome mat, there are compelling reasons why you must minister to them anyway.

1. Jesus commands us to love the unlovable. Jesus says: "For if you love those who love you, what reward have you? Do not even the tax gatherers do the same? . . .Therefore you are to be perfect, as your Heavenly Father is perfect" (Matt. 5:46, 48). The true test of love is loving people who don't love back.

2. Jesus came to seek and save the lost, and caustic kids are as lost as they can be. "Seek" is the key word here. Caustic kids need you to take the initiative. They're so lost they think they're okay when they're really self-destructing.

Jesus asked the scribes and Pharisees, "What man among you, if he has 100 sheep and has lost 1 of them, does not leave the 99 in the open pasture, and go after the one which is lost until he finds it?" (Luke 15:4)

Buddy Scott in *Group* magazine, September, 1990, paraphrases Jesus' answer: "I say to you that likewise, there will be more joy in heaven over one caustic kid who repents than over ninety-nine model kids who need no repentance."

3. Few adults have the maturity and perspective to love unlikable kids. Those who do have this ability are rare and precious. They can literally help turn a young person's life around.

4. Your ministry is the last hope for many caustic kids. If the church rejects troublemakers, the only group left for them to join is "the wrong crowd." This is the truth: Whoever values your kids most, and shows it, usually wins them over.

5. Deviant kids look for ways to justify their antisocial behavior. If you reject these kids, they'll use your rejection to justify their wrongdoing.

6. Caustic kids are hypersensitive about being treated unfairly. Troubled kids often judge an adult's worth by how fair he or she is. That's why it's imperative that you respond to your troublemakers fairly. It may not be fair for them to expect fairness from you, but they will, nevertheless.

7. Troublemakers aren't as tough as they seem. Caustic kids are ripe for ministry when they get into trouble. Many are genuinely afraid of what might happen to them. So don't bruise the fruit the way one Houston minister did. He got permission to visit a teenager at a drug treatment center. The first thing he said was: "I'm here to ask you one question. Are you the one who stole the hubcaps off my car?"

Blunders like this one explain why many health-care workers cast a suspicious eye toward people in the ministry.

8. You may know the "what" of their behavior, but you may not know the "why." Beneath the crusty surface of caustic kids may be enormous pain and frustration. When you minister to them instead of rejecting them, you give them the benefit of the doubt.

9. Strong-willed kids are tomorrow's leaders. Compliant kids are easier to minister to, but they may not accomplish nearly as much with what you teach them. Reach a strong-willed teenager and he or she will multiply your ministry many times over.

10. Ministry to tough kids keeps you from going soft. Kids who love you, hug you, and hang on to your every word make ministry *fun* for you. But tough kids will make ministry *challenging* for you. They keep you digging, praying, reading books, sharing with other youth leaders and, above all, they keep you growing.

It's time to relabel caustic kids as "lost kids." Lost kids are arrogantly self-destructive, blindly ego-centered, dangerously unconcerned about their rejection of Christianity, and rude to those who are trying to rescue them. In short, lost kids are proud of what they should be ashamed of. They need your help.

Deal with your prejudice against strong-willed kids. History shows that countless strong-willed kids who were channeled in the right direction grew up to save nations from tyranny and people from hopelessness.

Develop individual ministries to kids who are creating disasters in the group. If your youth group has been damaged by lost kids, you won't be surprised to learn that "caustic" has the same root as the "-caust" in "holocaust." You're compelled to minister to them, but you're not compelled to let them destroy your ministry. It's a fine line.

If lost young people pose a serious threat to the youth group, pull them out of the group setting and minister to them individually. Do this only after meeting with parents and pastoral staff to develop a "united front" for rescuing the kids while protecting the youth group.

Caustic youth take a long time. Conditions will probably get worse before they get better. To be effective, the relationship must be long term.

Caustic youth require you to change your expectations. Usually things will not turn out the way you thought they would. Here are some expectations that must change:

1. Caustic kids will appreciate you.
2. Caustic kids will trust you.
3. Caustic kids will obey you.
4. Caustic kids will be honest with you.
5. Caustic kids will be open to the Gospel.
6. Caustic kids will want to change.
7. Caustic kids will accept your values.
8. Caustic kids will accept your advice.
9. Caustic kids will become responsible.

10. Caustic kids will want to be loved.

Building relationships and communicating with caustic kids is not easy, but we really shouldn't expect it to be. First Corinthians 13:7 states that love "always protects, always trusts, always hopes, always perseveres." This kind of love involves paying the price, trusting, and having realistic expectations and commitment. It will be tough, but God calls us to nothing less then selfless love over the long haul. And *he* will change lives through you.

BRICK WALL YOUTH GROUPS

Brick wall youth groups are youth groups filled with caustic kids. They are stubborn, or-nery, rude, and produce a pervasive group spirit that's negative, cynical, and sarcastic. No matter what you do or say, kids mock and challenge you. A brick wall group seems to take pride in the number of youth leaders it can force into early retirement. The fright-ening thing about a brick wall group is that it scares "good" youth group members away.

Discipline doesn't always work in a brick wall group. I tried. I talked to kids individu-ally. I held retreats on spiritual lukewarmness. The senior minister even talked with the group. But nothing worked.

WHAT CAN YOU DO?

Fortunately, quitting isn't the only way to deal with a brick wall group. Make your min-istry effective by following these tips:

• **Look to the future**—Don't expect a sudden turnaround. In fact, it will be painful for the first 12 to 18 months.

• **Pull out the key bricks**—Unfortunately a brick wall group doesn't have one or two hardened kids, but a wall full. Yet, a few bricks are key. Remove them, and the wall will fall down.

A way to determine which kids are key bricks is to ask yourself: "If the youth group gets noisy, who could tell the group to quiet down and the group would listen?" These are the leaders.

Now by pull out, I don't mean kick these kids out immediately. I mean pull kids aside and find out their chief concerns. I invited a few key bricks out for pizza and paid for it. I wanted to hear what these kids thought of the youth group. Most were surprisingly can-did. They told me what they liked and disliked. I even learned that many held a lot of hurt inside. Some felt rejected by the church or pushed into Christianity by their parents. Af-ter the pizza outing, these kids seemed more open.

• **Pray**—In Mark 9:14-29 the disciples run into a situation that seems impossible. But verse 29 shows there's something they can do. "'Only prayer can drive this kind out,' an-swered Jesus; 'nothing else can.'"

Hurt and hardness need the tender softness of God's Holy Spirit. And that comes by prayer. I prayed a lot for activities in my group to go well, but I didn't pray much for the kids who needed it. And that prayer would have taken care of all my other prayers.

• **Get adult support**—The biggest danger in working with a brick wall group is losing

YOUTH ROOM

"My parents gave me $5 to come. For $7.50, I'll go back home."

your self-confidence. You begin to think that you're a failure.

You need people around you to show you that you're not crazy. You *can* minister to kids. Find volunteers to help you.

KIDS WHO ARE IN TROUBLE WITH THE LAW

Here are some practical ways that youth workers can help young people (and families of those young people) who have gotten themselves in trouble with the law.

There are several ways youth workers can help. Let's begin, however, by considering the major obstacle that youth workers face in responding to situations of this nature.

Youth workers often can't help because they aren't told of the problem. It's not surprising that many parents choose to remain silent in hopes that their child (and the family) will be spared further embarrassment. Others are concerned that their son or daughter will be labeled "troublesome" or "delinquent." Unfortunately, some parents are more concerned about how they might be negatively perceived than about their child's welfare. Youth workers must continue to remind parents through meetings for parents and teenagers, newsletters, special parenting seminars, and in personal relationships that the youth staff is ready and eager to support them through the bad times as well as the good.

We can assist parents by learning about the juvenile justice system. Most parents have no idea how the courts handle kids. If parents are made aware through meetings and newsletters that we are familiar with the police and court systems, they will be more open to approaching us in a time of need.

Whether a teenager is apprehended for relatively minor crimes like shoplifting, or is suspected of having committed a more serious offense like rape, the legal procedure used by most states and counties follows the same pattern. Generally, when a suspected offender is arrested or brought in for questioning (whether to police headquarters or to a juvenile detention facility), an intake evaluation is completed. This includes gathering information from the arresting officer and the juvenile. In some instances, where no prior police record exists and the offense is relatively minor, a "lecture/release" might be deemed most appropriate. The young offender is given a warning and sent home. Otherwise, a probable cause hearing is set to determine whether sufficient evidence exists to justify continuance of the process. If probable cause is established, a trial date is set before a judge, or in certain situations, a judge and jury. If the judge and jury decide that the evidence proves guilt beyond reasonable doubt, then a disposition hearing is set. At the disposition hearing, and as a result of weighing all possibilities and recommendations, the judge will rule on what treatment or punitive measures the court will order.

During the entire process, some offenders will be detained in a juvenile facility because of prior offenses, severity of the crime, inability to post bond, unwillingness of parents to receive back into their custody a child they consider beyond their control, or any other factor that the court believes might prevent the juvenile from appearing in the next phase of the process. Many juvenile facilities (short-term detention and long-term treatment) welcome the involvement of clergy or church-related youth workers who desire to maintain a continuing relationship with young parishioners who have been institutionalized. Although some facilities require strict adherence to regular visiting-hour procedures, most will be flexible enough to accommodate a pastor or youth worker's schedule.

Rich Van Pelt, in an issue of *Youth Worker* journal suggests a few ways to maximize ministry to young people who are incarcerated.

1. Take time to understand the institution's policies, procedures, and activities so you can better understand the young offender's situation. Remember that for most kids, incarceration is a distressing situation, no matter how cynical or calm they appear on the surface.

2. Develop relationships with staff counselors and chaplains within the institution. You'll enjoy even greater freedom when those in charge see you as cooperative and trustworthy. Don't make assumptions about a facility simply because it is "secular." Through the years, I've been privileged to minister in institutional settings where the rehabilitative atmosphere was excellent. The chaplain's office may already be offering outstanding programs and resources that you can support. Above all, recognize that you are not in competition with the institutional staff. Your support of their efforts and their support of yours can really benefit kids.

3. Be aware of manipulative behaviors. The well-meaning but naive youth worker can be a prime target for the developing "con" to practice on. In their desperate search for understanding, love, and acceptance, teenagers often manipulate adults for their own ends. They may take advantage of your relationship to earn favor with other staff members. The orientation and training sessions offered by most institutions may help volunteers identify and confront manipulative attempts.

4. Learn to be a good listener. In institutions, kids are thrust into a suspicious environment. Fearful that anything they say can, may, and probably will be used against them, they often withdraw and allow relationships to be only superficial. Because you represent the "outside world" and because you may have an existing relationship with the inmate from your group, there is greater possibility for more intimate sharing.

5. Keep promises you make and don't make promises you may not be able to keep. If you say you're going to visit on a particular day, make every effort to be there. If you can't, call and make sure the teenagers gets your message and your apology. Be consistent and dependable.

6. Leave books, magazines, and tapes (if allowed) with the young person. Kids living in institutions generally have too much free time. They may welcome reading and listening material. *Campus Life* magazine is a proven favorite. If tape players are allowed, leave Christian tapes of contemporary music and messages. Your youth group may enjoy helping to provide these materials.

7. Be aware of the young person's need for non-sexual physical affection. In relating one-on-one, you can often provide support through touching and hugging.

ALCOHOLIC KIDS

The recovering (never recovered) youth has lived more life than many of us would ever want to see. They are both more and less mature than their peers. These kids will be in any youth group—no one church has the monopoly on the "good kids" who don't do drugs or alcohol. They have special needs which we must recognize and learn about. And in many—if not most—of our communities, there is a crying need for such ministry to be done.

Recent research indicates that as much as 10 percent of the entire United States population is chemically dependent. That's 24 million people, both kids and adults, who are addicted to alcohol, drugs, or both. None of these men and women, boys and girls, can find healing on their own from their addiction. They need treatment. In response to the growing awareness of alcohol and drug abuse, treatment centers have opened around the country in great numbers.

The National Institute of Alcoholism and Alcohol Abuse did a nationwide study of high school seniors, and the results are disturbing. In the average class of twenty kids, one drinks alcohol daily, one smokes marijuana daily, one has used cocaine in the last month, and twelve have consumed alcohol in the last month. By the time our kids graduate from high school, nine out of ten will have experimented with some mood-altering chemical—alcohol, marijuana, or worse. This pattern of behavior often intensifies in college, out of the suspicious gaze of Mom, Dad, school, and church.

Let's stop kidding ourselves; many of these kids are in our youth groups. And they are in need of our love, intervention, and long-term help. For a long time we in ministry have stuck our heads in the sand about the matter of addiction, continuing to believe that addicts are weak, disobedient to God's expressed commands, or simply no good. Perhaps we ought to save the moral judgements for something really worthwhile and work instead with the young people that God has given into our care who are trying to make it out of the hell of chemical dependency. If nothing else, a kid may come into our youth group who has begun his recovery, is really searching for Christ in his life, and needs our support rather than our disdain.

The kids in recovery have a great spiritual void once the drug that filled their lives and gave them meaning is gone. We have a unique opportunity to fill that void with the knowledge and love of God in Jesus Christ. Virtually every recovery program—including both Alcohol and Narcotics Anonymous—urges the addicted person to hand over his or her life to a Higher Power. Following this, the person must take a fearless moral inventory of what they have done under the control of chemicals, seek forgiveness both of God and of those who have been hurt by their actions, and move out into life seeking the peace and serenity that God alone can give. That is pretty heavy stuff for the average sixteen-year-old; but when kids come to grips with these principles, they are making a step toward maturity in Christ that their non-addicted peers may not yet even comprehend.

How shall we minister most effectively to recovering youth? These principles suggested by John Throop in the summer 1987 issue of *Youth Worker* may be of help to you:

Presence. After intervention has taken place with one of the members of your youth group, visit the youth in the hospital as soon as possible. If they are in outpatient care, see them at home. They need your support at this time more than ever. Just being there assures them of your love and care and support. The kids will be carrying around all the guilt they need; once that guilt begins surfacing, you'll be a valuable resource.

Prayer. Pray for your recovering members every day. They need God's help and presence one day at a time. Try to learn exactly where they are in their treatment so that your prayers can be targeted. They can fall away from recovery at any time; they remain in recovery by the sheer grace of God. Your prayers do make a difference.

Partnership. As more recovering youth join your group, pair them together for mutual support. Chances are they'll know one another from the AA/NA meetings, but in your youth group you can be much more explicitly spiritual.

Program. As you work with your recovering members, be on the lookout for kids who are at a spiritual point where they can share a testimony of what God has done in their lives. Regardless of the polish of these youths, the other members of your youth group will listen intently because of the integrity of the speaker. These kids can be a real encouragement to your other youth group members that it's okay to say no to drugs and alcohol.

It may also be helpful to bring members of your youth group to an open AA/NA meeting. Some of the groups are open to anyone to come and see what AA/NA is about; other meetings are for members only. In many communities, there is an AA/NA chapter that is made up specifically of teens. If there's an open meeting there, a group can learn a lot by attending.

It can be a great service to the community and a potential ministry for your congregation to house a teen AA/NA group. Some of your youth group members may well be part of such a meeting. You also extend a subtle invitation to the participants to come and join your youth group.

The field is fertile with young people coming out of the nightmare of alcohol and drug addiction and into the life of recovery. We must be ready to receive them with the kind of unconditional love that the father had for his prodigal son. These kids in recovery are sadder, wiser, still confused—but most of all sober. They know what it is to be forgiven. Now they need to know from us what it is to be loved.

"Oh no—the First Church youth van just pulled in!"

CHAPTER 14

VANDALISM

Unchurched kids had vandalized the building. They didn't take anything, but they did do considerable damage. They painted profane sayings all over the walls. They dumped garbage on the floors and smeared human feces in the restrooms. Plus, the vandals littered the church with empty Budweiser cans and Jack Daniels bottles.

This malicious damage can sicken and squelch teens' enthusiasm to reach out to unchurched kids. They feel discouraged. Why would kids do such a thing—especially to the "house of the Lord?" What influences a teenager to participate in such negative and damaging behavior?

Teenage vandals typically don't have healthy adult role models, good peer relationships, or good self-concepts. And they have little or no relationship with God or the church.

Sometimes we see the church building as the center of worship rather than the worship center. For example, Rich Van Pelt, in *Group's* October/November 1988 issue, remembered when church leaders decided to allow a community-based organization to use the church facilities during school hours. Other church members voiced their concern over the "probable" abuse of the facility.

This incident reminds me of the contrasting conviction in Joseph Aldrich's *Life-Style Evangelism*: "Your church should be the greatest garbage dump in town. A place where the broken, oppressed, misplaced, abandoned, and unloved peoples can come and find a 'family,' where they are accepted and loved . . . as is. 'As is' people are Jesus' kind of people. The Pharisees despised them. They still do . . . If your heart is not broken by broken people, you don't have Jesus' heart."

I don't mean when kids vandalize church property and get caught that we do nothing. We're to be good stewards over all the gifts that God gives us. But sometimes we seem better at caring for a building than we are at caring for people.

When kids vandalize church property and get caught, we have an incredible opportunity to flesh out Christ's love. How we respond will speak volumes about what's most important to us.

Take Doug Runyon, youth minister from Nashville, Tennessee, for example. He first met Brian when he came to the church to apologize for the red spray-painted scribblings on the side of the church building, a bus, and a car's headlights. The police caught Brian in the act and gave him a choice between juvenile court or apologizing and helping with the cleanup. He chose to apologize and help.

"Although a bit skeptical, I invited him along on our all-night outing that evening," says Doug. "He showed up with several friends. . . .That was a year and a half ago. His friends no longer come, but Brian is a regular." The group's love and acceptance kept him coming back.

Not all teenagers apologize for vandalizing a church. But you can find other opportunities to show love and acceptance.

First, know how your justice system works. Juvenile justice systems vary from state to state. Kids who vandalize church property are usually charged with criminal mischief—a misdemeanor in most states. Then a judge arbitrarily decides on a fine, incarceration, or probation, taking into account any prior history with the police and the recommendations of his or her staff.

When kids vandalize church property, some youth leaders turn over the situation to the authorities and completely wipe their hands of any further responsibility.

But one inner-city youth leader took a different approach. He testified against young thugs who beat him up and left him for dead. A jury found them guilty as charged and the judge handed down a sentence that included time in a correctional facility.

After hearing the sentence, the youth leader offered to serve the cumulative time that each of the boys was required to do. The bewildered judge denied his request. The youth minister then shared with the judge, jury, and accused young men and all others present in the courtroom about Jesus' precedent 2,000 years ago on a cross. Although still denied the privilege of taking their sentence, this youth leader regularly visited each of his young assailants in jail. They experienced the unconditional love of God in a way that few ever do.

Another way to respond to church vandals that allows kids to face the consequences is to suggest that the judge agree to restitution—making things right—as an option of punishment. Kids can work a certain number of hours to compensate for the damage they do. For example, they may do maintenance, janitorial or clerical work for the church they vandalize.

View the offense as an opportunity. But recognize that some kids turn their backs on the church. They may act hostile. Don't let that stop you from trying. Be creative. Brainstorm possible ways to move toward reconciliation with kids who vandalize your church property.

Trust the results of your efforts to "Him who is able to do immeasurably more than all we ask or imagine, according to His power that is at work within us" (Eph. 3:20).

What about the kid who vandalizes and never gets caught? Our first inclination may be to protect the teenager. But teenagers need to face the consequences of what they do.

Because every situation is unique, deal with kids on an individual basis. We can respond in different ways. Always start with prayer. And then try the following suggestions:

- confront the teenager directly;
- inform the teenager's parents;
- alert the legal authorities;

- use any combination of the above; or
- do nothing.

You may decide to alert legal authorities. Pressing charges isn't easy, especially when you pray for and work at restoring relationships with kids. But sometimes it's the most loving thing you can do.

Though he'd left the church more than an hour ago, youth worker Sammy Jenkins couldn't shake the feeling that Junior High Night was not quite over yet.

LEARNING-DISABLED KIDS

There are more than 4.3 million learning-disabled kids in the United States. And the number is growing. In ten years, the number of "special education" students in U.S. schools has increased by 20 percent.

One reason for this burgeoning segment of society is tied to the breakdown of U.S. families. More and more kids are victims of physical, psychological, and emotional abuse at home. Brian McNulty, executive director of special education in Colorado, says: "Ten years ago in Colorado there were 1,000 documented cases of child abuse. This year we had 10,000."

Still, the school system overlooks many kids with learning disabilities. And so does the church.

Youth groups subtly ostracize kids with learning problems. Disabilities range from emotional handicaps to mild mental retardation. And slow learners make many people feel uncomfortable.

Youth worker Jude Fouquier knows how hard it is to integrate slow learners into his group. But he's learned to do it. The first step requires acceptance.

Fouquier takes his cues from Jesus—who not only accepted, but sought out people on the fringes. Jesus spent time with epileptics, paralytics and people suffering from all kinds of diseases (Matt. 4:23-25). "Those (the fringe people) are the ones he seemed to draw in because their presence added something that he felt was missing," says Bill Wolfe, former director of senior high education for the United Methodist Board of Discipleship. "Fringe people have an insight into life that nobody else does."

Your group members can grow from that insight. Many young people don't have contact with slow learners because they're separated from them in school. And slow learners who've been separated from their peers often don't develop their social skills.

Fouquier first helps the adult sponsors and teenage leaders in his group learn how to accept learning-disabled kids. "When the youth group members see a leader accepting someone—and most of our leaders are cool and someone to look up to—they learn to accept that person," Fouquier says.

But acceptance doesn't happen overnight. Kids who feel uncomfortable around slow learners tend to release their anxiety through unguarded condescension and crude joking. If that happens, Fouquier has a private talk with those involved.

Because Fouquier's group includes several severely disabled kids, he also invites a special education professional to speak to his group. She helps the group understand slow learners and learn how to socialize with them.

Mondragon says it's not hard to spot slow learners. According to the American Academy of Child and Adolescent Psychiatry, kids with learning disabilities:

- don't understand the concept of time;
- can't distinguish right from left—for example, confusing "25" with "52" and "no" with "on";
- lack coordination when they walk or play sports;
- fail schoolwork because of poor reading, writing, or math skills;
- have trouble following instructions;
- easily lose things, such as books; and
- have difficulty remembering what someone has just said.

Just as you can pick out bright kids simply by talking with them, you can identify slow learners when you ask questions and listen. That's how Fouquier discovered that Leland and Xavier, two guys in his senior high group, are learning-disabled. "It's not just their learning, but their mentality," Fouquier says. "They act like junior high kids."

But not all learning disabilities are so obvious. Kathy is a cheerleader at her high school. She attends class regularly and gets average grades. But twice a week a tutor visits her home to help her with reading assignments. When Kathy takes a test that involves a lot of reading, she goes to the counseling office, where her counselor reads the questions to her.

It's easy to overlook dyslexia or other reading disabilities. So find out privately by asking new group members to read something aloud, or to write something about themselves.

And be sure to talk to the person who drops off or picks up kids you suspect are learning-disabled. If learning or behavior problems are apparent, approach the subject directly. If not, simply show you're interested in learning more about the new members and their families.

Parents usually want to discuss their child's special needs. And they can teach you how to work with their slow learner. Jim, for example, will ramble on and on. His family stops him by saying, "Jim, that's enough!" That may seem abrupt—even rude—to you, but Jim's parents know this is the best way to handle him.

WHEN A STUDENT IS EMBARRASSED TO READ ALOUD

Slow learners in the Sunday School setting need extra care and attention. Their fear as they enter your Sunday School class is that they will be embarrassed and humiliated just as they have been in school. Make sure they know they will not be called on in front of the group unless they want to be.

I had a slow learner in my group (we'll call him Bill) a few years ago. I think one of the reasons we got along so well was because we spent time together outside of class. I would meet with him and go over next week's Sunday School lesson in a casual manner over a Coke at a fastfood restaurant. Then in the class I would ask Bill questions we had discussed that he would feel comfortable answering. Bill felt great because he was able to participate and contribute. It's also important to remember that being a slow learner doesn't mean that a student is slow in all areas. Bill had a fairly quick wit and was a lot of fun to be around after you took the time to get to know him.

James Dobson, in *Dare to Discipline*, shares the following experience of the slow learner being forced to read out loud in class, a situation which can cause discipline problems if we are not sensitive to it.

> When the slow learner finally reaches high school, a year or two after he should have arrived, he usually finds even less tolerance for his difficulty. One mature tenth grader was referred to me because he announced he was dropping out of school. I asked him why he was quitting and he said, "I have been miserable ever since I was in the first grade. I've felt embarrassed and stupid every year. I've had to stand up and read, but I can't even understand a second grade book. You people have had your last chance to laugh at me. I'm getting out." I had to tell him I didn't blame him for the way he felt; his suffering was our responsibility.[23]

DISCOVERING GIFTS AND TALENTS

Try not to focus on "can't do's." Look for talents and abilities your learning-disabled kids can offer the group.

One of Fouquier's group members who's learning-disabled is a good athlete. He does mime and is talented in drama. So Fouquier encourages him to improve those skills.

Two brothers with learning disabilities in Mondragon's group enjoy helping him set up for youth group meetings. "And I let them," Mondragon says. "For example, if I need to go upstairs to get a movie screen, Tom is right behind me, ready to help."

Don't ignore inappropriate behavior. Decide what behavior is acceptable for each individual slow learner. Then stick with your decision. The slow learner's teachers or parents can help you decide what to expect of that individual.

Andrea, one of Fouquier's group members, constantly talked while he talked. When Fouquier told her to stop, she said she couldn't help it. He replied: "You can help it. Sit next to someone who won't talk to you." After that, Andrea settled down. She no longer interrupted him.

Be sensitive to the needs of your learning-disabled kids as you design activities. If you plan an activity that requires kids to read—and you have a dyslexic young person in your group—break the group into pairs. Pair the dyslexic person with a sensitive group member. Then have partners trade off reading portions of the assignment. This puts everyone on the same level, and allows the dyslexic person to feel like part of the group.

If you're planning to play softball and one of your young people has poor motor skills, use a larger-than-normal, mushy ball. This way, everyone will have equal difficulty playing the game because you've introduced a "handicap" that everyone must overcome.

Don't work with learning-disabled kids alone. Get others to help you. Terry, who's severely disabled, wanted to go to summer camp but couldn't take care of himself there. So Peter, an adult volunteer, offered to help him throughout the camp. Peter gave Terry the attention he needed. And the group enjoyed summer camp together.

Team up an enthusiastic slow learner and a shy intellectual for a youth group activity. Each will benefit from the gifts and talents of the other. But one word of caution: Be careful pairing up guys with girls. Slow learners who aren't socially adept easily develop crushes on those who pay special attention to them.

If you build community with the slow learners in your group, your teenagers will understand Jesus' ministry more fully. "Everybody has deficiencies in something," Wolfe says. "And learning disabilities aren't necessarily more critical than other limitations. We're all limited. We all need help."

Understand the causes of behavior problems. A slow learner who becomes bored or frustrated often acts up. Reward good behavior. Be liberal with praise, but make sure it's genuine.

APATHETIC KIDS

Another area that drives many youth group leaders up the wall is the "I don't care" attitude that affects so many youth groups.

Due to instant communications and a shrinking globe, today's young people are not apathetic out of ignorance. In fact, many do care deeply about the world, their families, their youth groups, and vital issues of life and death, right and wrong. But unlike youth of former generations, they feel they don't matter. When television graphically delivers news of bloody conflicts or starving children, when headlines shout about gang wars and random violence, when the pastor preaches the plight of unsaved millions, today's teenager asks, "What could I possibly do about all this?" Young people suffer from an identity crisis, a feeling of smallness in the midst of overwhelming challenges.

In the past, the parents and grandparents of young people dealt with issues that hit close to home. They had to help support the family or care for younger siblings and older relatives. Their contributions were concrete. But today's issues are often systemic, global, and catastrophic. As a result, teenagers feel powerless, and the only way they feel they can cope is to withdraw. Though they are criticized for being apathetic and selfish, this behavior isn't the result of self-preoccupation of a surface nature, but rather a deeply rooted struggle for competence and significance.

The situation has been echoed in the church. In the past, young people were part of the church body; there were no separate youth groups or youth ministries. Today the church may unwittingly contribute to teenagers' apathy. When the "adults" run the programs, young people are left on the sidelines — relegated to their own group of peers. Often ministry is done *to* them instead of *with* them. This also contributes to the feeling of helplessness that leads to apathy.

INSPIRE THEM TO GREATNESS

Our role as youth workers is clear. We must inspire young people to greatness, by helping young people see themselves as God's agents of change in this world. Provide them with a sense of calling that generates unparalleled enthusiasm for life.

In youth work we have mistakenly assumed that the best way to relate to young people is to provide them with various forms of entertainment. Maybe instead we should invite young people to accept the challenge to become heroes and change the world. By helping them believe that God has called them to participate in the remaking of society, we can inspire them to action and deliver them from the deadness of the spirit we call apathy.

How do you motivate the kids who come to youth group with the attitude: "I don't care what's going on in the rest of the world?" We need to give these kids a graphic idea of just how many hurting people there are in the world and help them to understand that they have the ability to make a difference in these hurting lives.

KIDS ARE APATHETIC BECAUSE CHURCHES ARE OUT OF TOUCH

High schoolers are apathetic because churches refuse to connect biblical truths to teenage realities. We have to rethink ministry to this group. "Rethinking" means meeting senior highers' real needs. And many youth ministries just aren't doing that.

According to the Search Institute study, "Effective Christian Education: A National Study of Protestant Congregations," one out of three churchgoing teenagers has had sexual intercourse by the eleventh or twelfth grade. Yet only 27 percent of Christian teenagers say their churches emphasize sex education.

Forty-two percent of churchgoing eleventh- and twelfth-graders admit to drinking alcohol six or more times within the past year, yet only 20 percent of kids say the church stresses drug and alcohol education.

Typically, youth ministers have strong opinions about what kids need. But how many know what kids want to talk about? You may be surprised by the issues high schoolers hunger to learn more about.

KIDS ARE APATHETIC BECAUSE THEY HAVE NO FRIENDS IN THE CHURCH

It's ironic that senior highers' number one interest is learning to make new friends, but few have friends at church. Only 38 percent of churchgoing teenagers feel that their church peers care about them. That means if you have twenty high schoolers in your youth group, twelve of them feel unsupported by other group members. It's difficult to pinpoint those twelve kids since many "look" like they fit in.

Close relationships at church appear to keep kids involved for a long time. Speaking at the Religious Research Association meeting, researcher Daniel Olson said if people have strong friendships within the church, they tend to continue attending church even when they become dissatisfied with various aspects of church life.

Peer relationships are crucial for senior highers, but so are relationships with adults. "Churches can offer adolescents something available almost nowhere else in our culture: the interest, support, and care of adults," writes researcher Dorothy Williams in Search Institute's newsletter, *Source*. "Nowhere else are there as many opportunities for interaction between people of widely different ages."

KIDS ARE APATHETIC BECAUSE OF SENIORITIS (GRADUATION)

Churches can drive away senior highers by the very programming they think keeps young people involved. Many churches implement a rigorous education program for young people until a certain age. When the training is finished, most churches accept the kids as full-fledged members. In theory, this practice is supposed to increase kids' commitment to the church. But in reality, it often gives kids the message that once they've finished this training, they've "graduated" from church.

This "graduation mentality" is particularly true of churches that confirm teenagers. Confirmation (a structured program to prepare young people to join the church) becomes graduation to a lot of kids. After the confirmation, you start to see these kids twice a year, at Christmas and Easter.

Search Institute researchers also found this trend in their study. "Two denominations (the Evangelical Lutheran Church in America and the United Church of Christ) with strong emphasis on thorough study in preparation for confirmation retain their levels of participation of youth in grades seven through nine," reports the Search Institute study. "However, for both of those denominations, percentages of participation for youth in grades ten through twelve . . . drop well below the participation rates of all other denominations."

To address this problem, some churches hold their membership ceremonies for senior highers in the fall instead of the spring. That way, confirmation graduation doesn't overlap with high school graduation. It's harder this way for kids to link confirmation to "being on my own."

Other churches emphasize a long-term Christian education group. The programs for older teenagers and adults are just as exciting and challenging as the ones for younger kids.

KIDS ARE APATHETIC BECAUSE CHURCH IS BORING

Christian education alone won't generate excitement for peripheral high schoolers. It's got to be lively Christian education. Only 31 percent of churchgoing teenagers say church is interesting, reports the Search Institute study.

Although it is true that some youth will leave the church no matter how objectively exciting or meaningful it is, our concern should not be to blame those who have rejected the church, but to determine how we are part of the problem. The boring aspect of the church can be remedied relatively easily if a church is willing to make some changes.

Those changes include adopting an experiential learning approach in your group programming. Get senior highers moving, thinking, acting, laughing, crying or relating with others and you stand a good chance they won't be bored.

Boring programs invite misbehavior. I remember sitting in a convention of youth workers as a widely known writer spoke. Before he was through, however, nearly half of the youth workers had left because they were bored. The kids in our groups don't have the option of leaving when they get bored, so they simply look for other ways to entertain themselves.

I know we aren't in the church to entertain kids, but in this day of videos, electronic games, and highly visual concerts—not to mention good old omnipresent TV programming—we can't afford to be boring. If we're well prepared, know our subject, and present it in an interesting manner, discipline problems will be few indeed.

At the same time, youth workers need to explain to teens that most churches don't have video games and a Ferris wheel. Every part of church is boring sometimes. And some parts of church seem boring all the time. Of course, the same can be said for school, work and parades.

If church bores your teens, help them find ways to jazz it up. Encourage them to offer suggestions and volunteer their energy.

Did you ever hear a joke that wasn't funny until the punch line hit you later? Church can be like that. Kids won't always bounce out of the church doors on Sunday morning feeling spiritually revved up. In fact, some teens may leave wondering why they bothered going at all.

Sooner or later something will click inside their heads. That sermon, Bible story, or Sunday morning worship experience will speak directly to them.

KIDS ARE APATHETIC BECAUSE OF FEAR OF FAILURE

Fear of failure breeds apathy in teenagers. When faced with the social system's awesome demands to achieve—for grades, for trophies in sports, for popularity—many young people choose simply not to compete. Fearing failure, they find the easiest route is often simply to give up and declare they don't care.

One possible suggestion is to eliminate competition in your youth group. Caring youth workers will want to restructure their ministries and programs to provide some deliverance for teenagers who are stressed out by living in a highly competitive world. They will seek to provide an environment in which acceptance doesn't have to be earned, in which young people will feel loved without having to prove themselves.

Set up programs that don't encourage domination by super stars. Sports activities may seem like a healthy outlet for youth groups, but they are unhealthy if they simply become opportunities for the glorification of the already glorified or the degradation of the already put-down. Sensitive youth workers will encourage activities that neutralize the superior skills of some of the participants and that make having fun as a group the main purpose of recreation.

Tony Campolo in his book, *Growing Up in America,* tells of one youth worker who set up a volleyball game in which the net was fifteen feet high. Her youth group members played with a weather balloon instead of a volleyball, and the game was a crazy delight. Everyone participated as equals. The superjocks quickly learned that they couldn't dominate and that fun came from cheering the movement of a balloon more influenced by the wind then by their athletic prowess. Those who were not jocks quickly gained confidence as full-fledged particpants in the game. The game had everybody laughing, and winning was no big thing.

KIDS ARE APATHETIC BECAUSE THEY NEED SPIRITUAL REGENERATION

Apathy is also the natural condition of fallen humanity. It is only on unusual occasions that people are motivated to rise above the entropic state of being. M. Scott Peck, a Harvard psychotherapist, in his book *A Road Less Traveled,* contends that we are all basically lazy and too lethargic to make the life changes that will give us healthy dispositions and personal joy. Peck believes that it is only by God's grace that we can have the enthusiasm that dispels apathy. Isn't that what Paul said in Ephesians 2:4, "Because of His great love for us, God, who is rich in mercy, made us alive with Christ even when we were dead in our transgressions . . ."?

Our young people need spiritual regeneration to become young people who are wholly surrendered to what God wills to do in their lives. The Spirit gives life and without the Holy Spirit people are dead, apathetic.

This age, claimed Kierkegaard, can die, not from sin but from lack of passion. Passion for life is, ultimately, a gift from God. Let's challenge our young people and ourselves to rise from our apathetic morass and claim this most miraculous gift.

Every Youth Worker's Nightmare Come True

ATTENTION DEFICIT DISORDER KIDS

Some experts believe as many as 2 million kids have ADD. So chances are you have at least one junior higher or high schooler with ADD in your youth group.

Many doctors believe ADD is caused by a chemical imbalance in the brain. People with ADD have systems that don't function well without a certain neurotransmitter.

ADD is most often genetic in origin and is male dominant. ADD is found up to eight times as often in guys as in girls. The intensity of the symptoms vary from person to person. And there are still many unanswered questions about its causes.

Someone with ADD may have a short attention span or inability to stay on task, and problems maintaining concentration and responding quickly; this person may talk incessantly, or be distractible, impulsive, or hyperactive. However, not all people with ADD are hyperactive. ADD kids may appear irritable, impatient, easily upset, hard to discipline, and hard to please.

ADD is a complicated condition with many symptoms, so there are many ways ADD manifests itself. The different areas of manifestation are physical (hyperactivity), academic (inconsistent performance), behavioral (strong willed), emotional, and social.

The ADD youth acts before thinking, appears unable to organize his time, will perform tasks carelessly, and is often unable to complete assignments on time. Although ADD kids have average and sometimes above-average intelligence, they often struggle academically and socially, resulting in poor self-esteem.

Your understanding is crucial to helping an ADD kid be successful in your group. Insensitivity or ignorance will only reinforce an ADD kid's low self-esteem.

Find out from the parents what types of difficulties their teen experiences. Also find out his or her strengths and abilities. Then build on those strengths. If the kid is a poor reader, avoid calling on him to read aloud. Or, give him prior notice and allow him to prepare. If the kid is hyperactive, ask for his help in some project or make him your assistant. Keep the person busy and direct his energy positively.

Take the extra effort to find out what makes this kid different from the other kids. It takes time to develop relationships with these kids. Take time to get to know your kids with ADD. You could be the one to make a real difference in this young person's life.

ADD kids are accustomed to the love, acceptance and understanding from their family, but they don't always expect it or get it from other people.

You may know a kid who you suspect has ADD but has never been diagnosed. Talk to a trained counselor, educator, or doctor about your suspicions. Ask the expert what changes you need to make in a classroom setting to meet this young person's needs.

Let the parents know about your concerns. Encourage them to meet with the expert. Although parents are usually aware of problems with their kids, they may not be willing to admit the problem. Be patient. Parents have probably heard complaints for years and may not have known what to do or may deny the problem.

ADD kids are draining on their parents and others, but the rewards of accomodating them are worth the time and effort it takes to do so.

TEACHING THE ADD TEEN

Marlene LeFever, in the winter 1992 issue of *Youthworker* journal, gives the following practical steps for youth leaders to take in working with ADD kids.

• **Pray extra hard.** For the teens and for themselves that they will be able to help the young people, not add to their problems or lack of self-respect.

• **Use visual aids, small group activities, role-playing and other methods.** These activities demand tactile/kinesthetic participation.

• **Allow movement and some talking during class.** Counselor James Wiegand reports the words of a boy whose treatment was beginning to work: "You know, I used to talk all the time in class. The teacher would tell me to stop. I could for a little bit, but then before I knew it, I was talking again. This is the first time I have been able to stop talking when my teacher asked me to."

• **Provide structure while making concessions.** For example, the teacher who doesn't mind giving the teen extra time to finish assignments or even extending assignments beyond class time, is helping the ADD child.

• **Use a high level of touch.** The good teacher will touch the teen on the back or shoulder and have the abiltity to bridge the gap between having a relationship with the young person and the academic or Christian education process.

• **Have good eye contact.**

• **Have a good sense of humor.**

• **Be easygoing.** Willing to share the stories of their lives. Good ADD teachers are not so rigid and strict that they blow up if kids say something completely weird or out of context. Attention deficit kids often blurt out things without thinking. The traditional teacher tries to get the student to think in a predictable way, but the more experiential teacher flexes with the situation without reinforcing what is negative. The teacher might even laugh and say, "Well, this is a little off the wall." That kind of comment doesn't challenge or reprimand the ADD teens for who they are.

• **Be more loving than critical to both the teen and the parents.** Leaders have the responsibility to talk to parents about a potential problem. Although parents may be hearing the same message from other sources, someone from the church saying the same thing may carry extra weight.

• **Look for the good and be generous in positive reinforcement.**

THE ADD FAKE

What about the kid who is disruptive, and when you get ready to discipline them, yells out, "You can't discipline me because I have ADD." Is their ADD fake or real?

The diagnosis of ADD is not an excuse or defense for poor behavior. If a kid truly has ADD, that kid usually doesn't broadcast it. An ADD kid already has low self-esteem. Why would he or she want to risk others' ridicule? But if a kid claims that his behavior is a direct result of ADD, talk to that young person's parents. They may be able to confirm whether they've seen indicators of ADD or whether the person has been diagnosed with ADD.

Move from this conversation with a plan of action. Confront a "faker" and explain the truth about ADD. Tell the faker that while they may get a few laughs for their comments about ADD, someone who truly has ADD may cringe at their insensitivity and move further and further away from ever getting needed help.

WHEN YOU ARE IN OVER YOUR HEAD: REFERRALS

Support Groups for Attention Deficit Disorder:
Children and Adults With Attention Deficit Disorders (CHADDE)
499 N.W. 70th Ave., Suite 308
Plantation, Florida 33317
(305) 587-3700

Attention Deficit Disorder Association
8091 South Ireland Wy.
Aurora, CO 80016
(508) 462-0495

Association for Children and Adults with Learning Disabilites
4156 Library Rd.
Pittsburgh, PA 15234
(412) 341-8077

*"Our young people are away at their national convention.
So far the stats include three conversions, fourteen recommitments,
six minor injuries, and two counselor breakdowns."*

IT'S YOUR TURN

The final chapter of this book is very different from the seventeen which you have just read. In fact, it may be different from most things you have read on the subject of discipline. But I think you will find this chapter helpful and interesting.

After speaking on the subject of discipline to two separate youth conventions (one on the West Coast and one on the East Coast) with about 125 youth workers in each conference, I gave participants a chance to ask any questions about discipline situations in their own youth programs. The following transcript recounts the dialogue that took place.

Q: I came into a situation where I was trying to be everybody's friend. Now I want to set down rules. Is it too late?

A: It's not too late, but it will be difficult to lay down the law at this point. Sit down with your kids and talk about it. Have them help you draw up rules and consequences for breaking them. Mail a copy to the kids and their parents. Remember, if you don't tell them what the consequences are for breaking a rule, it's not fair. Here's an idea for keeping things light: at the end of a long list of rules I always add something funny. A few closing lines might be:

• If you don't follow these rules, you will have to wear bellbottom jeans or a plaid polyester suit with eight-inch lapels.

• If you violate these rules, you will be tied to a chair in front of a television and forced to watch reruns of Mr. Rogers.

• If you violate these rules, you will have to listen to Julio Iglesias or Barry Manilow tapes! (Sorry about that, but this list of rules was getting too serious.)

Q: This ninth-grader in my group is constantly talking. He's a smart kid, and I hate to kick him out of the Sunday School class. But right now he is really disruptive. How would you handle this?

A: First, you just have to get the student out of the class. Don't embarrass him; you may want to have another adult leader take him out of the class when he starts disrupting things. Then you'll need to confront him about his behavior. Let him know the consequences. If he is a person with leadership potential, you may want to get him personally

151

involved in the class or study by having him teach part of the lesson. Try to let him feel what a teacher goes through!

Q: At our weekly prayer meetings, the kids talk during the announcements. It's hard to control them during this time.

A: The best thing to do is try to make the announcements as fast and interesting as possible. Perhaps you could involve the students by having them make the announcements. Or put in a break or transition after the announcements and before the more quiet prayer time.

Q: How do you deal with kids who are disrespectful?

A: It's important to take time to talk to these students separately. You'll need to affirm that you love them, but that you cannot allow their behavior to go on. You may want to involve the parent. At any rate, you can't let the behavior go unconfronted. Choose a nonthreatening environment for your talk—such as a fast-food restaurant. Ask, "How can we prevent this from happening again?" Discuss the consequences for future misbehavior.

Q: At retreats, I've been very clear with rules and consequences. When the kids break the rules, I have to follow through with the consequences. But then I feel guilty about having to enforce the rules, and sometimes get repercussions from parents. Often I've backed off because of these feelings.

A: Sometimes you just have to live with the guilt. Bite the bullet and follow through. Yes, it is hard to confront kids, but dealing with a parent's anger can be much worse. Cover yourself. Be sure parents are fully informed of the rules before the retreat. When you have to discipline a young person, you may want to bring another adult sponsor along so a third party can "witness" your actions and help answer a parent's questions later.

Q: I have a group of junior highers who are always kicking and pulling at each other, giving each other "nougies," and so on. They also call each other names. How can I get them to cut down on this?

A: Sometimes a little clowning around is OK, especially when kids have been sitting still for long periods of time. Try to build this time into your meetings and have activities that let them "get it out of their systems." However, don't allow the students to put each other down with name-calling. Confront them individually about this behavior.

Q: We have a problem with older kids who drive; they want to run to the store or leave the meeting early. What should I do?

A: We have a rule that for group activities away from the church, only adults can drive. All the kids have to ride. The reasons are that there is always the possibility of accidents, and lack of unity can result when some kids drive to and from an activity. At the church, we can't stop them if they want to leave, but we do have a rule that they can't leave and come back. If they do leave the meeting, they have to go home; they can't mill around in the parking lot. You may need to tell the parents if some kids are causing a problem here. Remember to show them you care enough to give them rules.

Q: Do you ever limit the fun, social activities to kids who attend faithfully?

A: It depends on whether the activity is meant to be evangelistic or a reward. If it's an outreach, you can't expect non-Christian kids to attend all your other events. But I do have a program where kids are doing a special ministry project throughout the year, and each year we give a special event as a surprise reward. It's OK to do that as long as you aren't using the reward as a carrot to get kids involved in the first place: you want them to do ministry for its own sake.

Q: Sometimes we have a problem with kids and their music at special events. Do you set any rules about this?

A: Yes, we have a rule that, on retreats and trips, there can be no ghetto blasters. Walkmans are allowed if the volume is low enough to not be heard by others. One problem with Walkmans is that they leave group members too isolated. Sometimes on the way to a retreat, I encourage kids to leave the Walkmans off and enjoy each other and share with each other. But sometimes on the way back, when the kids are tired, it's OK for them to relax with their music. I encourage our young people to listen to Christian music. If there is a question on the type of music they are listening to, I talk to them privately about it.

Q: What do you do when you have a bus returning from Six Flags after a long day and one of the kids is late?

A: I would leave him. Of course, I've told the group four times very clearly what the departure time is. And I've made it clear to parents well in advance what will happen if kids are late—that they may be in for a drive of several hours to pick their child up. Now this is OK if you are at an amusement park which is supervised until closing time. It's a tougher decision if you are out of state or in an unsupervised area. Once I did leave a 12th grader in a national forest. But I knew him well enough to know he could handle the situation. And the rangers found him and helped him get back with his parents.

In ordinary circumstances when you can't leave a student behind, we usually take more than one vehicle. All the vehicles leave, but one will wait. If you only have one vehicle and absolutely have to wait, then you wait, delaying the entire group. But always call the parents, or a representative to go meet the parents at the pick-up point and let them know what is going on.

Q: What do you do about group members who have graduated but want to hang on?

A: I don't let them switch grades or keep attending after graduation. It's time for them to move into the college and career group even though they feel like small fish in a big pond. With kids who have been kept behind in school, this can be tough. But remember that, though they may be physically more mature than their peers, they may be emotionally and psychologically immature. You can rarely make an exception to this rule. For drop-outs . . . that's really hard. I often let them stay with the group they would have been in. After all, they need the help. But it can be difficult for them to obey the rules now that they are "out on their own."

Q: We have a problem with the deadlines for our retreat registrations. It's the parents who don't meet the deadline. What do you suggest?

A: You want to be consistent in how you handle these things. If they don't turn in the registration by the deadline, the student doesn't go. Sometimes you'll find the parents coming up with excuses for their kids, and that's why it's important to communicate with parents. I always send a letter and copy of the publicity for the event to the parents, explaining why it's important to have a registration cutoff date.

In some cases where my intended event is evangelistic and where I don't have to plan, I let kids sign up after the deadline with an extra cost tagged on. For other activities where an exact count is needed, I have a sign-up time for three weeks in a row and set the cutoff deadline for two weeks before the event—no exceptions.

Q: What about that age-old problem where you set a time to leave for a retreat or whatever, and kids are late?

A: Prepare ahead of time for that possibility. Communicate in advance that you will leave on time, and then follow through. You may want to set a time that you will meet at the church or elsewhere, without giving the specific time you will leave, giving yourself some leeway for latecomers, loading the buses, etc. In cases where kids want to leave the retreat early, or leave and come back, they can't do it. It disturbs the weekend. In some cases we do arrange for kids to come up a little later with a sponsor, but once they are there, they stay there.

Q: What would you do about a parent sponsor or chaperon who too harshly disciplines his or her own child on an outing? We had a case where, after a couple of warnings, the mother of a group member smacked the girl in front of everybody. It put a real damper on the mood of everyone, especially the girl.

A: When parents want to be involved as sponsors, I always try to make sure the kid wants the parent involved. Some parents have the wrong motives for "helping"—they are overprotective, or want to "spy" on their child, or even are too lenient. When a parent is involved and cracks down too hard on the child, I suggest you talk privately to the parent later and let her or him express feelings and reasons for the behavior. Take time also to encourage and affirm the child and help her understand what happened and why it occurred.

Q: We have a problem with kids talking when others are talking, and then saying "shut up" to each other. How do I put a stop to this?

A: Talk to each group member separately about the problem. Explain that you won't allow them to put each other down by telling each other to shut up. It is OK to encourage positive peer pressure in this type of situation.

Q: What do you mean by "positive peer pressure?"

A: That's where you allow the kids to participate in making the rules and do some policing of their peers. Again, you want to be developing self-discipline—that which comes from within. Be careful of using extrinsic motivation—punishments and rewards—too often. Extrinsic motivation works better with kids younger than junior-high age.

Q: One of my students has a parent who is abusive. If I discipline this student, the parent is likely to take it out on him. What should I do?

A: Whatever problem the student may cause, don't paint it too bleakly to the parent. Establish good communication with the parent—keeping him informed of both good and bad behavior. You may feel it's wise to allow the student a second chance before going to the parent, but don't wait too long. If the parent hears of the misbehavior through the grapevine instead of from you, he could be extra-hard on the child. When you are planning to talk to the parent, inform the child so he has some time to prepare the parent for your call.

Q: What kind of discipline would work best with my group, which has many unchurched kids from the inner city?

A: Try to be sensitive to individual needs. Do what you can to know and talk to parents, and discover ways to spend extra time with group members outside of regular meetings. Be aware that these kids won't respond to "Would Jesus want you to do this?" but may be responsive to positive peer pressure.

Q: You say that you love all the kids in your group. How do you love even those kids that are giving you real discipline problems?

A: It's not always easy, but loving kids is a decision you have to make. And confrontation can be a part of that love—in fact, it has to be part of it. You can "draw the line" in a way that shows love and concern for kids by supporting discipline with positive relationships.

NOTES

1. Fitzhugh Dodson, *How to Discipline with Love* (New York: Signet Books, 1978), 1.
2. Elizabeth Crisci, *What Do You do With Joe?* (Cincinnati: Standard Publishing, 1981).
3. Howard Hendricks, *Heaven Help the Home* (Wheaton, Ill.: Victor Books, 1973), 68.
4. C. Donald Cole in *Moody Monthly* (September 1976).
5. Robert C. Kolodny, et al., *How to Survive Your Adolescent's Adolescence* (Boston: Little, Brown and Company, 1984), 136.
6. Hendricks, *Heaven Help the Home*, 65.
7. Leonard Berkowitz, *The Development of Motives and Values in the Child* (New York: Basic Books, Inc., 1964), 55–56.
8. Bruce Narramore, *Help, I'm a Parent* (Grand Rapids: Zondervan, 1972), 41.
9. Gordon MacDonald, "The Difference between Discipline and Punishment," in *Parents and Teenagers*, ed. Jay Kesler (Wheaton, Illinois: Victor Books, 1984), 411.
10. Kenneth O. Gangel, "Discipline: A Family's Friend or Foe?" in *Parents and Teenagers*, 424–25.
11. J. S. Plant, quoted in Norma E. Cutts, *Better Home Discipline* (New York: Appleton-Century-Crofts, Inc., 1952), 288.
12. G. Keith Olson, *Counseling Teenagers* (Loveland, Colo.: Group Books, 1984), 36.
13. Dodson, *How to Discipline with Love*, 10.
14. Warren Bennis, "The Unconscious Conspiracy: Why Leaders Can't Lead," from *In Search of Excellence*, ed. Thomas J. Peters and Robert H. Waterman, Jr. (New York: Harper and Row Publishers, 1982), 59.
15. Ronald W. Tyrrell, Frederick Hanoch McCarty, and Frank A. Johns, *Growing Pains in the Classroom* (Reston, Va.: Reston Publishing Company, 1977), 94–95.
16. James Dobson, *Dare to Discipline* (Wheaton, Ill.: Tyndale House Publishers, 1970), 88.
17. Tyrrell et al., *Growing Pains in the Classroom*, 156–57.
18. *Parade*, January 18, 1987.
19. Paul Hauck, *How to Do What You Want to Do: The Art of Self Discipline* (Philadelphia: Westminster Press, 1976), 50.
20. Tyrrell, et al., *Growing Pains in the Classroom*, 93–94.
21. Haim G. Ginott, *Between Parent and Teenager* (New York: Avon Publishers, 1969), 90.
22. Warren W. Wiersbe, "Be Disciplined," in *Parents and Teenagers*, 411.
23. Dobson, *Dare to Discipline*, 141.

BIBLIOGRAPHY

Allen, Roger, and Ron Rose. *Common Sense Discipline*. Fort Worth: Sweet Publishing, 1986.

Apter, Steven J. *Troubled Children/Troubled System*. New York: Pergamon Press, 1982.

Benson, Dennis C., and Bill Wolfe. *The Basic Encyclopedia of Youth Ministry*. Loveland, Colo.: Group Books, 1981.

Bodenhamer, Gregory. *Back in Control*. Englewood Cliffs, N.J.: Prentice-Hall, 1983.

Buntman, Peter H., and Eleanor M. Saris. *How to Live with Your Teenager*. New York: Ballantine, 1982.

Bybee, Rodger W. *Violence, Values and Justice in the Schools*. Boston: Allyn and Bacon, 1982.

Canter, Lee, and Marlene Canter. *Assertive Discipline*. Santa Monica: Canter and Associates, Inc., 1984.

Chase, Betty N. *Discipline Them, Love Them*. Elgin, Ill.: David C. Cook Publishing Company, 1982.

Coleman, James S., et al. *Youth: Transition to Adulthood*. Chicago: University of Chicago Press, 1974.

Dobson, James. *Preparing for Adolescence*. New York: Bantam, 1980.

Elkind, David. *All Grown Up and No Place to Go*. Reading, Mass: Addison-Wesley, 1984.

Feldman, Ronald A., Timothy E. Caplinger, and John S. Wodarski. *The St. Louis Conundrum: The Effective Treatment of Antisocial Youths*. Englewood Cliffs, N.J.: Prentice-Hall, 1983.

Herron, Orley R. *Who Controls Your Child? Nashville: Thomas Nelson Publishers, 1980.*

Ingersoll, Barbara. *Your Hyperactive Child*. New York: Doubleday Publishers, 1988.

Kesler, Jay, ed. *Parents and Teenagers*. Wheaton, Ill.: Victor Books, 1984.

Kesler, Jay, and Ben Sharpton. *When Kids Are Apathetic*. Elgin, Ill.: David C. Cook Publishing, 1991.

Kolodny, Robert C., Nancy J. Kolodny, Thomas E. Bratter, and Cheryl A. Deep. *How to Survive Your Adolescent's Adolescence*. Boston: Little, Brown and Company, 1984.

Leshan, Eda. *When Your Child Drives You Crazy*. New York: St. Martin's Press, 1985.

Lipsitz, Joan. *Growing Up Forgotten*. New Brunswick, N.J.: Transaction Books, 1977.

Martin, Grant. *The Hyperactive Child*. Wheaton, Ill.: Victor Books, 1992.

Offer, Daniel, et al. *The Adolescent: A Psychological Self-Portrait*. New York: Basic Books, 1981.

Olson, G. Keith. *Counseling Teenagers*. Loveland, Colo.: Group Books, 1984.

Page, Joy P. *When Parents Cry*. Denver, Colo.: Accent Books, 1980.

Rice, Wayne. *Junior High Ministry*. Grand Rapids, Mich.: Zondervan, 1978.

Rosenzweig, Susan, and Kathleen Dunleavy. *Early Adolescence: A Resource Directory*. Center of Early Adolescence, 1986.

Seltzer, Vivian C. *Adolescent Social Development: Dynamic Functional Interaction*. Lexington, Mass.: Lexington Books, 1982.

Silver, Larry. *The Misunderstood Child*, 2d ed. Blue Ridge Summit, Pa.: TAB Books, 1991.

Spotts, Dwight, and David Veerman. *Reaching Out to Troubled Youth*, rev. ed. Wheaton, Ill.: Victor Books, 1994.

Sprick, Randall S. *Discipline in the Classroom*. West Nyack, N.Y.: The Center for Applied Research in Education, 1985.

Strack, Jay. *Good Kids Who Do Bad Things*. Dallas: Word Publishing, 1993.

van Pelt, Rich. *Intensive Care*. Grand Rapids: Zondervan Publishing, 1988.

Wender, Paul. *The Hyperactive Child, Adolescent, and Adult: Attention Deficit Disorder through the Lifespan*. New York: Oxford University Press.

Wilson, Earl D. *You Try Being a Teenager*. Portland, Oreg.: Multnomah Press, 1982.

Woodson, Robert L. *A Summons to Life: Mediating Structures and the Prevention of Youth Crime*. Cambridge, Mass.: Ballinger Publishing Company, 1981.